Mark Foley

UPPER INTERMEDIATE

Total English

Workbook (with key)

PEARSON
Longman

Contents

Reading

1 **a** Read the text about *Friends*. Match the descriptions A–E with the paragraphs 1–5.

A Explains the background and content of *Friends*. ☐

B Describes some negative reactions to the show. ☐

C Introduces us to the theme. ☐

D Gives factual information about the *Friends* series. ☐

E Explains the success of the show in an international context. ☐

b Read the text again. Answer the questions.

1 Were any of the main actors in *Friends* famous before the show began?

2 Was the show popular in the early days?

3 Who invented the show?

4 Why do people like the characters in *Friends*?

5 What creates most of the comedy in the show?

6 Which two features made it hard to believe in the characters?

7 How did the producers try to keep the show interesting?

8 What was missing by the end of the series?

c Find words and phrases in the text that mean:

1 make a lot of money (*adj*, para 2)
_____

2 was suggested formally/put forward (*v*, para 2) _____

3 equal to/the same as (*n*, para 2)
_____

4 statistics which show how many people watch something (*n*, para 3) _____

5 a group of television stations which covers an entire country (*n*, para 3) _____

6 watched a particular TV station (*phr v*, para 3) _____

7 ask for and receive (*v*, para 3)
_____

8 attractive and appealing (*adj*, para 4)
_____

9 something that unifies people (*n*, para 4)
_____

10 lost its energy (*phrase*, para 5)
_____

The F·R·I·E·N·D·S Phenomenon

1 Everybody loves their friends. But do you love *Friends*? If you are one of the half a billion people that have seen this hugely popular American TV show then the answer is probably 'yes'.

2 By far the most successful and profitable comedy series of recent times, *Friends* has been shown in more than thirty countries around the world. The series has been nominated for a record number of forty-four Emmys, American TV's equivalent of the Oscars. The previously unknown actors who play the main characters are now international household names and multi-millionaires.

3 First shown in the USA in 1994, the show quickly became a favourite with the viewing public, achieving top ratings for American television network NBC. 238 episodes were recorded and when the final episode was shown in 2004 more than fifty-two million people tuned in to watch. The show became so popular that by the time of the ninth series each of its six stars was able to command a fee of £1 million *per episode*!

4 The brainchild of writers Marta Kauffman and David Crane, the series follows the romantic and personal adventures of a group of six friends in their twenties and early thirties living in New York city. Kauffman and Crane were careful to create a cast of believable characters that almost everybody can identify with. Like real people, each of the characters has both endearing and irritating qualities. They are very different from each other, but share a common bond in their friendship and loyalty. It is the interaction between these contrasting personalities that provides most of the humour in the show.

5 Although popular with the public, *Friends* has not always been a hit with the critics. Some found it hard to believe in these young people who, although supposedly doing very ordinary jobs, seemed to lead lives of endless leisure in unfeasibly large apartments. And it didn't escape notice that over the years the producers began to become more and more dependent on bringing in new characters and guest stars in order to keep the show fresh. As a result there seemed to be an endless stream of new or ex-boyfriends and girlfriends appearing. The focus on the six main characters, which had provided the magic ingredient in the show's early success, began to be lost. Most critics agreed that by the tenth series the show had run out of steam and the announcement that episode number 238 would be the last came as no great surprise.

Writing

2 a Read the messages 1–3. Match them with the writers A–C.

A a work colleague ☐
B a friend ☐
C a neighbour ☐

①

Bill
Thanks for agreeing to feed the cats!
The cat food is on the top shelf in the cupboard.
And don't forget to give them some water.
I'm back on Thursday.
Jerry

②

Party tonight at 9 p.m.
The garden flat at 82 Mandeville Road.
It is just behind a big Supersaver supermarket.
Bring some nice food!
Millie   X X

③

for: Darren
mes: Harriet from the Accounts Department called at 3 o'clock.
Please email her the figures for the Smithson account before tomorrow morning.
Her email is harriet.donald@smiths.org.ur
Tricia

b In notes and messages we often leave out unnecessary words. <u>Underline</u> at least five words in each message which we can leave out.

Grammar | question tags

3 Complete the sentences with the correct question tags.

1 We should have waited longer, _____?
2 Mr Bolton couldn't come, _____?
3 Hardly anybody writes letters now, _____?
4 Let's get a pizza this evening, _____?
5 You went to Greece last summer, _____?
6 Nothing works on this computer, _____?
7 You won't forget to ring me, _____?
8 Nobody answered the advert, _____?
9 Help yourself to a drink, _____?
10 I'm late again, _____?

4 Five of the questions tags are incorrect. Tick (✓) the correct sentences and correct the mistakes in the others.

1 Nobody likes cabbage, does he?
2 Let's get a taxi this time, shall we?
3 You can't use a mobile phone on the plane, can't you?
4 Somebody told you, didn't he?
5 Leave the keys under the mat, will you?
6 Hilary isn't married, isn't she?
7 Nothing's expensive in this shop, are they?
8 Take one of my business cards, will you?

Pronunciation

5 a 🔲1.1 Cover the tapescript. Listen to ten sentences and mark the intonation of the question tags rising (R) or falling (F).

1 ____   6 ____
2 ____   7 ____
3 ____   8 ____
4 ____   9 ____
5 ____   10 ____

b Listen again and choose the best explanation A–D for each sentence.

A The speaker expects the listener to agree.
B The speaker isn't sure about the answer.
C The speaker wants the listener to do something.
D The speaker is making a suggestion or offer.

1 ____   6 ____
2 ____   7 ____
3 ____   8 ____
4 ____   9 ____
5 ____   10 ____

TAPESCRIPT

1 We can't smoke in here, can we?
2 Take a copy of the brochure, won't you?
3 It doesn't open until midnight, does it?
4 Nobody likes her, do they?
5 Let's try that new Thai restaurant, shall we?
6 The weather's awful today, isn't it?
7 Put the keys back when you've finished, will you?
8 I'm next in the queue, aren't I?
9 Those designer sunglasses are terribly expensive, aren't they?
10 Get me a glass of water, will you?

Listening

1 **a** `1.2` Cover the tapescript. Listen to an extract from a radio programme and choose the best title.

1 The Recent History of Juggling

2 Different Types of Juggling around the World

3 Juggling in Ancient Times

b Listen again and mark the statements true (T) or false (F).

1 David Stourton is a juggler. ☐

2 Professional jugglers use the term 'toss juggling'. ☐

3 The earliest picture of jugglers is from ancient China. ☐

4 There is a picture of Egyptian jugglers in a museum in Berlin. ☐

5 There is no evidence of juggling in the Americas. ☐

6 Tagatus Ursus was a Roman juggler. ☐

7 There were probably jugglers in Ireland in ancient times. ☐

8 Jugglers were usually also clowns or jesters. ☐

c Now read the tapescript and find words that mean:

1 writer of a particular book _____

2 throwing _____

3 a place where someone is buried _____

4 metal weapons with sharp blades _____

5 restricted to one area _____

6 something that shows where somebody is buried (2 words) _____ _____

7 spoken stories about the ancient past _____

8 connected _____

TAPESCRIPT

Woman:	On today's *Meet the Author* we're talking to David Stourton, author of *A Short History of Juggling*. David, welcome to the programme.
David:	Thanks.
Woman:	Now, I suppose we all have a broad idea of what juggling is, but could you tell us what **you** mean by 'juggling'?
David:	Sure. I pretty much stuck to the traditional idea of juggling. I think the dictionary calls it 'keeping two or more objects in the air at one time by alternately tossing and catching them'. In the profession we call that 'toss juggling'. I think that's the type of juggling most people are familiar with.
Woman:	Has juggling been around for a long time?
David:	Oh yes. I found references to juggling from more than 3000 years ago. There are some Egyptian tomb paintings which show jugglers from the Middle Kingdom period, and there's an ancient Egyptian statue of a juggler in the Staatliche museum in Berlin.
Woman:	What about written records?
David:	Well, the earliest written record that we know of is from ancient China. There's a book from the 3rd or 4th century BC which describes a juggler who could throw seven swords in the air.
Woman:	That sounds like something from one of those Chinese martial arts movies!
David:	Yes, juggling with swords is a well-established tradition in the Far East.
Woman:	So was juggling confined to the Middle East and Asia in ancient times?
David:	Not at all. There were lots of jugglers in ancient Rome. We even know the name of one of them, Tagatus Ursus.
Woman:	Did the Romans juggle with knives, like the Chinese?
David:	Probably not. We know that Tagatus Ursus juggled glass balls, because they're specifically mentioned on his grave stone. And, interestingly, when the Spanish discovered the Americas, they noted in their reports and diaries that the Aztecs had jugglers.
Woman:	Are there any records of juggling here in Britain?
David:	Well, not exactly, but jugglers are mentioned in several of the Irish and Norse myths, which date from the fifth to the twelfth centuries. Of course, by the time of the Middle Ages there are plenty of references to jugglers in Britain.
Woman:	You talk about jugglers as if they were part of an actual profession. I mean, is that really the case?
David:	It's hard to say with any certainty. In some cases jugglers were also clowns or jesters, or even acrobats.
Woman:	Yes, I can see how the skills might be linked. Now, can you tell us about the more recent history of juggling ...

Grammar | *any/every/no/some*

2 Complete the text using words from the box.

> all anybody anything everybody
> everything nothing only some
> somebody something

Goodbye to CDs

In the old days the (1) _____ way to get your favourite pop song was to walk into a record shop and buy a CD. But (2) _____ stays still in the world of technology and when you talk to young people today it seems they are (3) _____ getting their music from the Internet, with the result that many record stores are experiencing dropping sales and can often be virtually deserted.

Nowadays it seems (4) _____ is downloading songs as digital files from the Internet and listening to them on MP3 players and mobile phones. (5) _____ who still buys their music from shops is regarded as a dinosaur!

In fact in Britain the 'pop chart' – the list of the most popular songs – is now based equally on sales in shops and on the number of songs downloaded from the Internet. Record companies have recognised the importance of this new way of distributing music and (6) _____ you could possibly want to hear is now available in digital form. From the latest avant-garde groups to the most obscure medieval church music, there is always (7) _____ ready and willing to record even the most esoteric piece of music and upload it onto the Net.

Of course, (8) _____ that can be downloaded to one computer can also be downloaded to another, so it's easy to swap music tracks with your friends. But (9) _____ musicians aren't happy with this situation. Making illegal copies of tracks deprives them of royalties. They believe (10) _____ should be done to prevent what they feel is little more than downright theft.

3 Rewrite the sentences using a single word to replace the phrases in *italics*. Make any grammatical changes that are necessary.

There are *no good programmes* to watch on TV.
There is nothing to watch on TV.

1 *None of the contestants* won any prizes.
_____

2 Would you like *a glass* of water?
_____

3 We've been through *all the files* and we can't find your application form.
_____

4 I'm sorry but we haven't got *any hotel rooms* available in July.
_____

5 *All the people* in my street own cars.
_____

6 I waited at reception for ages but I couldn't find *a single person* to help me.
_____

7 We've got lots of silk dresses but I'm afraid we have *no silk dresses* in your size.
_____

8 Jane always has *a number of* flowers in her flat.
_____

Vocabulary | making adjectives from nouns

4 Complete the missing word in each sentence.

1 My nephew's very a_____c. He loves painting.
2 I am r_____e for our after-sales service.
3 Ice-skating well requires great s_____l.
4 Never underestimate the i_____e of having good friends.
5 Dorotea runs a very s_____l business.
6 People in big cities are often more l_____y than people in small towns.
7 I've got very big feet so I often get f_____d when I'm trying to buy shoes.
8 Albert Einstein was famous for his incredible i_____t.

How to ... | agree/disagree

5 Match the sentence halves to make expressions of agreement/disagreement.

1 That's absolutely   a at all.
2 I completely   b in that.
3 I'm not sure if   c right.
4 That's not true   d completely true.
5 I don't think that's   e I agree with that.
6 I think there's some truth f agree with that.

Listening

1 a **1.3** Cover the tapescript. Listen to the dialogues 1–4 and match them with the situations A–D.

A on a train ☐   C a survey ☐
B in a shop ☐   D in a café ☐

b The following statements are factually incorrect. Listen again and correct the mistakes.

Dialogue 1

1 The man only uses his phone to send text messages.

2 He's able to use his phone at work.

Dialogue 2

3 The man expects train journeys to be noisy.

4 The woman thinks it's expensive to make mobile phone calls.

Dialogue 3

5 Steve's mobile was expensive.

6 John doesn't think Steve's new phone is very good.

Dialogue 4

7 The customer doesn't have any children.

8 If he isn't happy after ten days, the customer can get a different phone.

c Now read the tapescript. Find the words and phrases 1–10 and match them with the meanings a–j.

1 non-stop ☐
2 drives me mad ☐
3 more money than sense ☐
4 cost a bomb ☐
5 tarrifs ☐
6 on special offer ☐
7 tracks ☐
8 the really neat thing ☐
9 loads ☐
10 keep in touch ☐

a for sale at a reduced price
b maintain contact with somebody when you are physically separated
c songs or short pieces of music
d a large quantity
e all the time
f have lots of money but not very much intelligence
g prices for using a service
h makes me very angry
i very expensive
j something particularly impressive

TAPESCRIPT

1

W: Excuse me. We're doing a survey on mobile phones. Could I ask you a few questions?

M: Sure.

W: Do you own a mobile phone?

M: Yes.

W: And what do you mainly use it for?

M: Sending text messages, I suppose.

W: How many would you send on an average day?

M: Well, about five or six usually.

W: And are those mainly for business or social purposes?

M: Oh, just social. I can't use my phone at work – I'm an airline pilot.

2

M: Honestly. You want some peace and quiet and all you hear is those awful mobile phones non-stop. It drives me mad!

W: Yeah, and people talk such rubbish, don't they? 'Er, I'm on the train, and now we're pulling in at a station ...'

M: Some of these people must have more money than sense. It must cost a bomb to make all those calls.

W: Maybe they're on one of those 'cheap daytime calls' tarrifs.

3

J: Is that a new mobile Steve?

S: Yeah. I got it on special offer.

J: It looks very sophisticated.

S: Mm. It was really good value. It's got a camera and it can play MP3 files.

J: So you can listen to all the latest tracks...

S: Exactly. But the really neat thing is that it's got this special text messaging service that gives you all the latest football results. *You* should get one, John. They had loads of them in stock.

4

W: Which model are you interested in, sir?

M: Well, I'm not sure. But I want a phone that takes photos.

W: OK. Most of them do that now anyway.

M: Oh, right. Well, I like to keep in touch with the kids when I'm abroad, so I need a phone that works in other countries.

W: In that case, you need a 'triband' phone then. Anything else?

M: Yes, I want something that's really small and light, you know, easy to carry around.

W: Well, what about this Minirola? We have a ten day trial period policy here. If you're not happy with it, you could bring it back and we'll return your money.

The Miracle Chip

Scientists at Imperial College London today announced plans to begin full-scale trials of a new device which (1) ___ revolutionise the lives of people with serious medical conditions. The device is a miniature sensor less than two millimetres square which (2) ___ monitor changes in the body and is able to send out warning signals via a mobile phone.

The sensor, a microprocessor, is put under the skin of a patient's body and (3) ___ detect any dangerous changes long before the patient is even aware of them. This means that patients with serious conditions who would usually have to stay in hospital (4) ___ now live at home and (5) ___ lead more or less normal lives.

When it detects changes in the body, the microprocessor sends out a pre-programmed text message to the patient's doctor or hospital, describing the changes in detail. Of course, patients with the device (6) ___ carry their mobile phone with them at all times, but this will be the only restriction on their lifestyles.

Although it will probably be expensive to develop, the device (7) ___ be a boon to the economy because those patients who (8) ___ work because of the need to be near medical facilities will be able to go back to full-time employment, saving the government millions in sickness and unemployment benefits.

The first patients to be given the implant will be diabetics, but doctors hope to extend the trial to those with heart or lung diseases. And in years to come the device (9) ___ be adapted to cover even more conditions.

If all goes to plan and the trial is a success, the device (10) ___ be available to the general public within three to four years.

Vocabulary | noises

2 **1.4** Listen to the sounds 1–6 and complete the sentences with appropriate words.

1   Does your dog _____ at the vacuum cleaner? Mine does!
2   I _____ when I saw a spider in the bath.
3   The walls are so thin we can hear our neighbour's phone _____.
4   Our house is very old so all the floors _____.
5   She was so angry she _____ her fist on the table.
6   The dictionary fell to the floor with a loud _____.

Grammar | present/future modals of possibility

3 The tapescript for Ex. 1 contains several modal verbs. Look at the extracts 1–6 and match them with the meanings a–f.

Dialogue 1
1   *Could* I ask you a few questions? ☐
2   I *can't* use my phone at work ☐

Dialogue 2
3   It *must* cost a bomb ☐

Dialogue 3
4   It's got a camera and it can play MP3 files ☐
5   You *should* get one ☐

Dialogue 4
6   you *could* bring it back ☐

a   describing an ability
b   asking for permission
c   giving advice
d   describing a future possibility
e   saying that something isn't allowed
f   making a strong prediction

4 Read the text. Choose the best words to complete it.

	A		B		C	
1	A	must	B	could	C	can't
2	A	can	B	might	C	may
3	A	can't	B	can	C	might
4	A	can	B	must	C	should
5	A	can	B	must	C	can't
6	A	may	B	could	C	must
7	A	can't	B	could	C	must
8	A	can't	B	could	C	can
9	A	might	B	can	C	can't
10	A	can	B	couldn't	C	should

Review and consolidation unit 1

Vocabulary

1   Use the clues to complete the crossword.

Across

1   I'm on the same ___ as her; we feel the same way about things.
6   He made a good ___ on his new boss.
9   She isn't married but she's got a ___.
10 She's perfect for you. I'm sure you'll ___ with her.
11 I don't see eye to ___ with my sister.
12 He's an old friend; we are very ___.

Down

2   I don't know him well. He's only an ___.
3   He's the son of my mother's new husband. He's my ___-brother.
4   They'd been married for ten years before his ___ got sick.
5   Clare's a ___ of mine – we both work in the travel agency.
7   We're inseparable; I feel he's my real ___.
8   I've got two ___-sisters from my mother's previous marriage.

Question tags

2   Choose the correct alternative.

1   Somebody has been using my toothbrush, *haven't they/hasn't he*?
2   I'm going to be late, *aren't/are* I?
3   Let's book online, *shan't/shall* we?
4   They could have phoned, *could have/couldn't* they?
5   Miranda never eats meat, *doesn't/does* she?
6   *Something/Nothing* needs to be done, doesn't it?
7   We hardly ever go to the theatre, *don't/do* we?
    Have a piece of cake, *haven't/won't* you?

any/every/no/some

3   Tick (✓) the sentences which are possible and put a cross (✗) by the sentences which are incorrect. Sometimes both are possible or incorrect.

1   A   I wasn't able to find anything to fit me. ☐
    B   I wasn't able to find nothing to fit me. ☐
2   A   Would you like any dessert? ☐
    B   Would you like some dessert? ☐
3   A   There's anything wrong with this phone. ☐
    B   There's something wrong with this phone. ☐
4   A   Everything on the list were unavailable. ☐
    B   Anything on the list were unavailable. ☐
5   A   Did anyone call while I was out? ☐
    B   Did someone call while I was out? ☐
6   A   I've tried anything. It still doesn't work. ☐
    B   I've tried everything. It still doesn't work. ☐
7   A   There's nowhere to store things in my flat. ☐
    B   There are nowhere to store things in my flat. ☐
8   A   We're bored; we haven't got everything to do. ☐
    B   We're bored; we haven't got anything to do. ☐

Vocabulary

4   Complete the text using words from the box. Four of the words are not needed.

> artistic   importance   important   intellectual   jealous   loneliness   lonely   responsibility   responsible   skill   success   successful

I come from quite a large family. The great thing about a large family is that you never feel (1) _____ because there's always someone to talk to.

My elder brother, James, is a university professor. He's very (2) _____; his hobby is reading Greek philosophy! I'm the (3) _____ one in the family. I'm a graphic designer. My twin brother, Martin, is the practical one. He's a carpenter and he can do amazing things with wood. It's a (4) _____ I really admire.

But my younger sister, Kate, is the most (5) _____ of us all; she's the managing director of a huge company. She has the ultimate (6) _____ for more than 250 workers. Of course, she earns an enormous salary which we are all a little (7) _____ of! But in the end money doesn't matter. The (8) _____ thing is that we all support each other.

5 Use words from the box to complete the sentences. Change the forms as necessary. Two of the words are not needed.

> crash bark snore ring
> creak scream thud bang

1 Bob's _____ kept me awake all night!
2 Katrina _____ when she saw the accident.
3 I hate dogs that _____ all the time.
4 Put some oil on that door; it _____ whenever you open it.
5 Please don't _____ the door when you leave!
6 My mobile doesn't _____, it vibrates.

Present/Future modals of possibility

6 Choose the correct words to complete the dialogue.

Jim: Where are the children? They're not in the bedroom.

Sue: I'm not sure. They (1) ___ be playing in the garage.

Jim: No, they (2) ___ be there – it's locked.

Sue: Oh, they (3) ___ be in the garden then. There's nowhere else.

Jim: OK. I'll have a look. (*Two minutes later*) Well, they aren't there.

Sue: I suppose they (4) ___ be next door, although it's unlikely.

Jim: No, they (5) ___ be there. The neighbours are on holiday.

Sue: You're right. What about the park? They (6) ___ be there.

Jim: But the park is closed on Sunday afternoons.

Sue: That's not true. You (7) ___ go there until six o'clock.

Jim: Well, perhaps we should go and get them.

Sue: Yes, we (8) ___ take your car.

Jim: No, we (9) ___. I lent it to my sister.

Sue: Oh yes. I forgot. Well, let's ask John, he (10) ___ lend us his car.

1	A	can	B	might	C	must
2	A	can't	B	mustn't	C	might
3	A	could	B	must	C	can't
4	A	can't	B	mustn't	C	could
5	A	must	B	can't	C	might
6	A	can	B	might	C	couldn't
7	A	must	B	might	C	can
8	A	can't	B	could	C	couldn't
9	A	can't	B	might	C	must
10	A	couldn't	B	must	C	might

Vocabulary

7 Use suitable forms of the phrasal verbs in the box to finish the second sentence of each pair so that it has the same meaning as the first sentence.

> bring up fall out get on go out with
> look up to show off split up take after

1 Brenda and Lucy have a good relationship.
Brenda _____ with Lucy.
2 I've always admired my grandmother.
I've always _____ my grandmother.
3 It can't be easy raising three children on your own.
_____ three children on your own can't be easy.
4 Michael and Jane have ended their relationship.
Michael and Jane _____.
5 Why does your brother try to impress us all the time?
Why does your brother _____ all the time?
6 Surinda looks just like her mother.
Surinda _____ her mother.
7 I've had an argument with my best friend and I'm not speaking to him any more.
I _____ with my best friend.
8 Henry's having a relationship with one of the girls in his office.
Henry _____ one of the girls in his office.

Listening

1 **a** **[2.1]** Cover the tapescript. Listen to four people talking about their jobs. Match the speakers 1–4 with the jobs in the box. Four of the jobs are not needed.

> ballet dancer   engineer   secretary
> actor   architect   photographer
> journalist   hotel receptionist

1 _____
2 _____
3 _____
4 _____

b Listen again and complete the expressions 1–8. Then match the expressions with the definitions a–h.

Speaker 1

1 I'm a natural _____, I suppose. ☐
2 There's a sort of _____ that you get from an audience.

Speaker 2

3 I never meant to get into this _____. ☐
4 ... it all sort of _____ from there. ☐
5 But I'm _____ so basically ... ☐

Speaker 3

6 ... some of the guests are _____! ☐

Speaker 4

7 I had _____ space ships and futuristic cities for some reason. ☐
8 ... designing is something that's _____. ☐

a   difficult to manage/deal with
b   person who likes to be the centre of attention
c   an obsession with
d   developed/grew rapidly
e   career or profession
f   part of your basic personality
g   feeling of excitement
h   self-employed

c Complete the tapescript using appropriate future forms of the verbs in the box. Then listen and check.

> appear   take   leave   live

TAPESCRIPT

1

I'm a natural show off, I suppose. Even as a kid I loved performing in front of other people. Whenever the family got together my parents used to get me to stand on the table, singing songs and doing little scenes. There's a sort of buzz that you get from an audience that nothing else quite matches up to. In fact, I _____ on stage again next month, which should make a nice change from all the TV work.

2

It all happened by accident, really. I mean – I never meant to get into this line of work. In fact, when I was young I wanted to be a ballerina! But when I was at university a friend persuaded me to take some pictures for the college magazine, and it all sort of snowballed from there. The fashion shoots are the ones I enjoy most. But I'm freelance so basically I _____ any assignment that's on offer. Even weddings!

3

The really great thing about my job is the number and variety of people you meet. Not that they are all nice – some of the guests are a real handful! But however bad they are, you always know that they _____ in a few days, so that makes it bearable. And of course, I often get the chance to use my languages.

4

Even when I was quite small I loved drawing. I had a thing for space ships and futuristic cities for some reason! Well, of course, I don't really do any actual drawing now – the computers do it all for us! But designing is something that's in the blood, and the great thing about my job is that it's not just theoretical, because you know real people _____ and work in the things you've designed ...

Vocabulary | verb phrases about work

2 Complete the sentences using appropriate forms of the expressions in the box. Two of the expressions are not needed.

> be a people person
> be able to meet tight deadlines
> be good at using your own initiative
> be good with figures   be made redundant
> be promoted   do voluntary work
> get the best out of other people
> have a 'can do' attitude
> ~~have an eye for detail~~
> keep calm under pressure
> take early retirement   work well in a team

Jane's really good at seeing all the small things in documents and reports.

Jane *has an eye for detail.*

1 It doesn't matter how rushed he is, Javier always gets things finished in time.
Javier _____.

2 Working with Selema is great. She always seems to encourage her colleagues to do well.
Selema _____.

3 Even when things are really hectic, Dimitri is able to stay relaxed.
Dimitri _____.

4 Henrietta is at her best when she is huddled over her calculator working on numbers.
Henrietta _____.

5 My mother helps at the local old people's home, although she doesn't get paid.
My mother _____.

6 Alison is so positive, she thinks anything is possible.
Alison _____.

7 George really excels when he is working as part of a group.
George _____.

8 Clare wanted to travel so she left work when she was only fifty-five.
Clare _____.

9 You never need to give Rachel any guidance. She always manages to think of what to do on her own.
Rachel _____.

10 After working as a salesman for ten years, Fernando has at last been made sales manager.
Fernando _____.

Grammar | futures overview

3 Complete the sentences using appropriate forms of the words in brackets.

1 I'm not really sure but I think I _____ the Caesar salad. (try)

2 We're so excited about our holiday – we _____ the Taj Mahal! (see)

3 The meeting _____ at ten tomorrow so please be here by nine-thirty. (start)

4 No thanks, I'm full up. I _____ any more. (think/not/have)

5 Peter hates buses so he _____ by car. (probably/come)

6 The company _____ the new factory on January 1st next year. (open)

7 Look at those dark clouds, I think there _____ a storm. (be)

8 Mia's very well qualified so she _____ to get the job. (be/bound)

9 I can't see you next Tuesday because I _____ a conference. (attend)

10 We haven't set an exact date but the wedding _____ sometime in the spring. (definitely/be)

How to ... | talk about future plans

4 Use the word prompts to write about your future plans and predictions/ideas.
think/have/bath/this evening.
I think I'll have a bath this evening.

1 have decided/start/do/exercise
_____

2 not sure about/buy/that jacket
_____

3 plan on/have/lie-in/Sunday
_____

4 bound/get/marry/one day
_____

5 probably/not win/lottery
_____

6 like/have/holiday
_____

Reading

1 **a** Read the text. Answer the questions.

1 What does the word *guilt* in the title refer to?

2 Why is the weight of the sculpture significant?

3 What happens to 90% of Europe's electronic waste?

b Read the text again and find two more examples of each of the following types of vocabulary.

Adjectives	Adverbs	Parts of the human body	Electronic equipment	Domestic appliances
terrifying	*ingeniously*	*head*	*computers*	*cookers*

c Find words or phrases in the text that mean:

1 thrown away (*adj*, para 1) _____

2 when somebody paid an artist to make a particular work (*v*, para 1) _____

3 wasteful (*adj*, para 1) _____

4 advanced technology (*compound adj*, para 1) _____

5 wires connecting electrical appliances (*n*, para 2) _____

6 devices held in your hand which control computers (*n*, para 2) _____

7 promote/persuade (*v*, para 3) _____

8 at the present time (*adv*, para 3) _____

9 places where rubbish is stored and then covered over with earth (*compound n*, para 3) _____

10 burned (*v*, para 3) _____

Sculpture of Guilt

(1) This is 'Weee Man', a terrifying metal and plastic sculpture created by Paul Bonomini from discarded computers, electronic components and domestic products. Commissioned by the Royal Society of Arts (RSA), the sculpture stands 24 feet (7 metres) high beside the river Thames in London and serves as a shocking reminder of the huge amount of waste produced by today's extravagant high-tech society.

(2) The main body of the figure includes twelve washing machines, ten fridges, seven vacuum cleaners, thirty-five mobile phones and twelve kettles, plus assorted microwaves, televisions, radiators and sections of ducting and cabling. The artist has ingeniously created the head from a combination of surprising elements. The teeth are in fact computer mice, the eyes are washing machine doors and the ears are satellite dishes.

(3) The name of the sculpture, 'Weee', comes from the phrase Waste Electrical and Electronic Equipment, and its weight, 3.3 tonnes, is the same as the weight of electrical equipment thrown away by an average person in a lifetime. The RSA hopes that the sculpture will encourage recycling by dramatically reminding us of the sheer quantity of products we throw away unnecessarily. Citizens of the European Union currently produce 6.5 million tonnes of electronic waste a year, most of which ends up in landfill sites or is incinerated. A mere 10% is recycled.

Grammar | Future Perfect and Future Continuous

2 Use the prompts to write answers to the questions. Use appropriate forms of the Future Perfect or Future Continuous.

A: Will you have finished work by five-thirty tomorrow?

B: No, I/not finish/until six

No, I won't have finished until six.

1 A: Will you be going on holiday next July?
B: No, I/go/in August instead

_____

_____

2 A: Do you think Henry will have finished the project by the time I get back?
B: Yes, he/should/finish/it by then

_____

_____

3 A: Will Mr Simpson be able to see me between four and five?
B: No, I'm afraid he/see/another client then

_____

_____

4 A: Can we start work on the building site next January?
B: Yes, we/should/receive/planning permission/by then

_____

_____

5 A: Will the children be joining you for the summer?
B: Yes, they/stay/with us from July to September

_____

_____

6 A: Can we meet in the office tomorrow afternoon?
B: No, I/work/at home/all day tomorrow

_____

_____

7 A: How are you getting on with the decorating?
B: Pretty well. By the end of next month we should/finish/most of it

_____

_____

8 A: Will Gabriella's report be ready for the meeting this afternoon?
B: Yes, she/do/it by lunchtime at the latest

_____

_____

3 Complete the mini-dialogues using the Future Perfect or Future Continuous forms of the verbs in brackets.

1 A: Can I watch the cartoons now, Mum?
B: No. You can wait until after dinner.
A: But they will've by then! (finish)

2 A: Do you think we'll get there in time?
B: No, I don't. By the time we get there the train _____. (leave)

3 A: Next week's going to be really busy.
B: Not for me! This time next week I _____ on a beach in Sardinia. (lie)

4 A: Is Deirdre coming to the party on her own?
B: No. She _____ her boyfriend. (bring)

5 A: I don't want to spend hours waiting for her at the airport.
B: Don't worry. I'm sure Jan _____ by the time we get there. (arrive)

Pronunciation

4 **a** **2.2** Look at the examples of *have* in sentences A and B. Is the pronunciation the same or different? Listen and check.

A I won't <u>have</u> a coffee, I'd prefer a glass of water.

B I won't <u>have</u> finished by then.

b **2.3** Look at the following sentences and decide if the pronunciation of *have* is the same as A or B above. Then listen and check.

1 She didn't <u>have</u> the silk one, it was too expensive.
2 She will <u>have</u> done it by the end of the week.
3 I'll <u>have</u> the fried chicken please.
4 Will you <u>have</u> fixed it by the time I get back?
5 They won't <u>have</u> heard the news in time.

Vocabulary | 'after work' activities

5 Four of the sentences contain mistakes. Tick (✓) the correct sentences and correct the mistakes in the others.

1 At the weekends I like to social with my friends.
2 A good way to meet new people is to make evening classes.
3 It's important to spend quality time for your children.
4 My sister's going to study for a degree online.
5 By the end of the month we'll have finished redecorating the kitchen.
6 You should always try to keep up to day with your emails.

Reading

1 **a** Read the newspaper extracts. <u>Underline</u> all the examples of forms of the word *work* in the headlines. Mark the examples adjective (adj), noun (n) or phrasal verb (phr v).

A

New report claims shift work can damage health

A report published today claims shift workers suffer from significantly worse health than those working regular hours. Scientists in Frankfurt examined 400 factory workers, half of whom worked regular night shifts, and compared their health with regular office staff.

B

Car makers reduce work force by 10,000

A leading Japanese car maker has announced massive redundancies at its Birmingham plant. Half of the 20,000 workers are likely to lose their jobs. A spokesman for Hon-Tang Automotive explained that disappointing sales of its new saloon car were to blame for the decision.

C

'I work out twice a week' admits overweight TV star

Len Travis, star of television's hit series *Fight the Flab*, has admitted he exercises regularly at a gym in West London. Len, 45, was spotted by a press reporter while leaving the exclusive health club. The overweight actor had previously claimed that he never did any exercise and was 'a total sloth'.

D

Workaholic partners blamed for 40% of failed marriages

Sociologists at an American university have found that more than a third of divorces are caused by partners spending too little time at home. 'Some husbands or wives can be obsessed with work, spending as much as 50 hours a week away from home,' claims senior researcher Carol Dimkins.

E

Government working on new mobile phone regulations

The Ministry of Science and Technology is planning to introduce new laws governing the use of mobile phones. A committee of civil servants has been developing a series of new regulations designed to prevent the misuse of phones by children. Their proposals are likely to include the banning of all mobiles at schools and colleges.

F

'I'm still working class' claims millionaire rock star

Zed Taylor, lead singer with Canadian rock group The Zeds, has been defending his social background in a recent TV interview. Despite earning over $4 million last year and owning homes in Los Angeles and Vancouver the singer, 32, says he is still the same as when he grew up in one of the poorest neighbourhoods of Toronto.

b Read the list of dictionary entries which all contain the word *work*. Match the definitions with the words in the box.

> shift work   work ethic   work force
> work load   work on something
> work out   work permit   work station
> workaholic   working class
> workmanship   work-shy

1 _____ (*phr v*) to spend time working in order to produce or repair something.

2 _____ (*n*) a belief in the moral value and importance of work.

3 _____ (*phr v*) to make your body fit and strong by doing exercises.

4 _____ (*adj*) someone who avoids working because they don't like it.

5 _____ (*n*) somebody who chooses to work a lot, so that they don't have time to do anything else.

6 _____ (*n*) all the people who work in a particular industry or company.

7 _____ (*n*) the amount of work that a person or organisation has to do.

8 _____ (*n*) the group of people in society who traditionally do physical work and do not have much money or power.

9 _____ (*n*) When workers work for a particular time during the day or night and are then replaced by others so that there are always people working.

10 _____ (*n*) skill in making things, especially in a way that makes them look good.

11 _____ (*n*) an official document that you need if you want to work in a foreign country.

12 _____ (*n*) the desk, usually with a computer, where an office worker works.

Grammar | *in case*

2 Rewrite the sentences using *in case*.

We thought we might have to wait a long time so we took lots of books.

We took lots of books in case we had to wait a long time.

1 Maria took plenty of toys because she thought the children might get bored.

_____

_____

2 We're going to get extra copies of the keys made because we could lose one.

_____

_____

3 They may deliver the parcel this morning so please listen for the doorbell.

_____

_____

4 Leave your mobile turned on because I might need to contact you.

_____

_____

5 I thought the food on the train might be too expensive so I took some sandwiches.

_____

_____

6 Glasses often get broken so you should take your spare pair.

_____

_____

7 We might meet someone famous so we're taking our autograph book with us.

_____

_____

8 There was a chance of rain so they packed a couple of umbrellas.

_____

_____

Writing

3 This letter contains ten words or phrases which are unsuitable in a job application. Replace the underlined mistakes with more appropriate words or phrases. Look at page 28 of the Students' Book to help you.

79 Great Gorton Way
Hambley WW6 89X
Tel: 01234567890

14 April 2007

Martin Brewster
Head of Human Resources
Mega Travel Ltd
PO Box 899
Edinburgh
E12 YUT

Dear (1) Head

I am writing to (2) make application for the job of trainee travel agent (3) advertised by this week's *Jobs Weekly*.

(4) I think travel's really interesting and I have visited several foreign countries in the last three or four years. I feel (5) I'd be very good for the job because I have considerable personal experience of the problems travellers face in foreign countries. When I was in Mexico last year I helped two English tourists who had lost their travel tickets, and this (6) motivated me to feel very confident about myself.

I have just completed my degree in Modern Languages at Hambley University. I can speak (7) really good Spanish and Italian and I have a reasonable knowledge of French and Portuguese.
(8) I have a fantastic knowledge of the tourist resorts in southern Europe. I believe this would be a considerable advantage to a trainee travel agent in your company.

I am 22 years old. I live in Hambley at the moment but I would (9) be OK about moving to Edinburgh if I was offered the job.
(10) You can call me on my mobile phone number above at any time.

Yours sincerely

Danny Kingston

Danny Kingston

Vocabulary

1 Use the clues to complete the crossword.

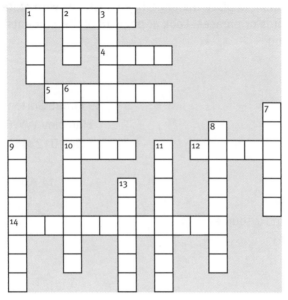

Across

1 She loves company. She's a ___ person.
4 He knows how to get the ___ out of people.
5 Dan's an accountant so he's good with ___.
10 I like company. I work well in a ___.
12 You must be able to meet ___ deadlines.
14 He enjoys his work. He gets a lot of job ___.

Down

1 Doctors follow a very strict career ___.
2 I'm going to take a year ___ between jobs.
3 It wasn't just a job, it was a ___ of love.
6 Candidates must use their own ___.
7 He's very precise. He has a real eye for ___.
8 Ana's very sympathetic. She's a good ___.
9 You must always keep calm under ___.
11 I want workers with a 'can-do' ___.
13 I'm fed up at work. It's time for a ___ of career.

2 Choose the correct alternative.

1 Miranda's been on *illness*/*sick* leave for the last three weeks.
2 He's only fifty but he's decided to take early *retirement*/*retiring* from his job.
3 Peter *does*/*makes* a good living as an independent financial consultant.
4 They have been *at*/*on* strike since Thursday.
5 Caroline does shift *job*/*work* so she sometimes has to sleep during the day.
6 They closed down the factory and *made*/*did* my uncle redundant.
7 Jeffrey has been *raised*/*promoted* to manager.
8 David told me he has resigned *of*/*from* his job.

Futures overview

3 Choose the best way to complete each sentence.

1 I won't be able to see you tomorrow because
   A I go to the hairdresser's.
   B I'm going to the hairdresser's.
2 Look at the damage on these tyres;
   A they aren't going to last much longer.
   B they aren't lasting much longer.
3 I'm not very thirsty;
   A I think I won't have anything to drink.
   B I don't think I'll have anything to drink.
4 David's such a good engineer –
   A I hope he'll get the job.
   B I hope he's getting the job.
5 Tania's just given me the tickets –
   A we're sitting in the front row.
   B we're going to sit in the front row.
6 That young pianist seems so talented;
   A I believe he'll win the competition.
   B I believe he's winning the competition.

Future Perfect and Future Continuous

4 Complete the sentences using a Future Perfect or Future Continuous form of a verb from the box. Use the pronoun *you* if necessary.

> ask   finish   watch   repair
> sunbathe   travel   clean   visit

1 Maria _____ all the rooms by the time the guests arrive.
2 By this time next week I _____ on a beach in the Maldives.
3 _____ your brother play football on Saturday?
4 Do you think the engineer _____ my computer by this afternoon?
5 By the end of the journey she _____ more than 20000 miles.
6 _____ preparing those figures in time for the directors' meeting?
7 _____ your half-sister while you're in the States?
8 During the lunch break tomorrow I _____ everybody to fill in a special questionnaire.

Vocabulary

5 Match the diary entries 1–5 with the descriptions a–f. One of the descriptions is not needed.

Monday	meet Dave, Liz and Sue for dinner at restaurant 8 p.m. ① ___
Tuesday	Internet café – find hotels in Venice ② ___
Wednesday	painting all day ③ ___
Thursday	Internet café – module 6 of accountancy course ④ ___
Friday	take Zoe and Bob to the zoo 9.30 – 12.00 ⑤ ___
Sat~~urday~~	

a visit chat rooms
b socialise with friends
c do research on the Internet
d study for a qualification online
e spend quality time with your children
f redecorate the kitchen

in case

6 Complete the sentences using *in case*.

1 I put on some insect repellant _____ _____.

2 You'd better take an umbrella _____ _____.

3 I always keep some aspirin _____ _____.

4 I think you should put on some sun cream _____ _____.

5 You should take a map _____ _____.

Vocabulary

7 There are eight mistakes in the text. Find the mistakes and correct them.

I think one of the most important things in life is being happy at work. I'm a website designer and I remember that when I applied to my current job I told the interviewer I
5 wasn't just keen of design, I was passionate on it! Perhaps that's one of the reasons I got the job. I suppose I'm quite lucky because not only do I love my work, I also get on really well with my colleagues. They are all very
10 different at me, but we all believe to what we are doing, so there's a great team spirit in the office. I work for a big advertising agency. It's a very busy and competitive business. Some of my colleagues worry of that but I just get
15 on and do my work. I think I'm pretty good of what I do and I'm really proud in some of the work I've done for the company.

Listening

1　**a** `3.1` Cover the tapescript. Listen to an extract from a radio programme about epic films. Complete the table with a number or word.

Hollywood's greatest historical epics

Film/Year	Notes
Gladiator 2000	• earned more than (1) $_____ at the box office
Ben Hur (2) ____	• (3) _____ by William Wyler
Spartacus (4) ____	
El Cid (5) ____	• the story of (6) _____ hero Rodrigo Diaz
Lawrence of Arabia 1962	• featuring a young Irish (7) _____
Cleopatra (8) _____	• (9) _____ Elizabeth Taylor
Troy (10) _____	

b Listen again. Which film is the speaker talking about?

1　perhaps the greatest epic of them all _____

2　Ridley Scott's inspiration for *Gladiator* _____

3　the most expensive film ever made at the time _____

4　disappointing box office _____

5　almost bankrupted its makers _____

6　went on to win five Oscars _____

c Now read the tapescript. Find the words and phrases in the text that mean:

1　being ignored/sleeping _____

2　type _____

3　look at something a second or third time _____

4　period of greatness _____

5　buildings created for a film _____

6　excellent _____

7　together with _____

8　huge amount of money _____

9　number of people paying to see a film _____

10　actors in a film who don't speak _____

TAPESCRIPT

1

One of the most remarkable developments in the recent history of film-making (1) _____ the revival of the historical epic. After lying dormant for almost forty years, this spectacular and lavish genre of film-making (2) _____ an unexpected reappearance with Ridley Scott's *Gladiator* in 2000. When it went on to win five Oscars and to earn over $458 million at the box office, Hollywood was forced to re-examine this area of film-making.

2

So, what exactly is a historical epic? To explain that we have to go back to the late 1950s and the film that marked the start of the brief golden age of the epic, *Ben Hur*. *Ben Hur* (3) _____ all the classic ingredients of the historical epic. It was long, it was set in a long distant period of history, it featured lots of battles, and it had big stars and even bigger sets. Directed by William Wyler and released in 1959, the film (4) _____ six years to make and had cost $15 million – the most expensive film ever made at the time. But it went on to gain eleven Oscars and huge profits for MGM.

3

There followed a series of superb epic films. In 1960 there (5) _____ legendary director Stanley Kubrick's powerful *Spartacus*, starring Kirk Douglas and Lawrence Olivier – the film that was in fact Ridley Scott's inspiration for *Gladiator*. The next year Charlton Heston, the star of *Ben Hur*, (6) _____ alongside Sophia Loren in *El Cid*, the moving story of Spanish hero Rodrigo Diaz's attempts to drive the Moors out of Spain. 1962 saw the release of perhaps the greatest epic of them all, David Lean's *Lawrence of Arabia*, featuring a young Irish actor who (7) _____ on screen before, Peter O'Toole.

4

The end of this short golden age (8) _____ in 1963 with the release of *Cleopatra*. Directed by Joseph L Mankiewicz and starring Elizabeth Taylor, the film had cost a fortune to make and was never able to make a profit at the box office. By the early 1960s, television (9) _____ to eclipse films, cinema attendances were falling and the amounts of money film makers (10) _____ were simply too small to cover the enormous production costs of historical epics.

5

This changed with the advent of computer generated imaging, or CGI as it is known, in the late 1990s. Suddenly it was possible to have as many soldiers and horses, Roman arenas and Trojan city walls as you wanted, without having to pay extras or build huge sets. But with the disappointing box office for Wolfgang Petersen's *Troy* of 2004 and Oliver Stone's *Alexander* of 2005, perhaps this second golden age of the historical epic may also prove to be short-lived.

Grammar | narrative tenses

2 Look at the tapescript for Ex. 1 again. Complete the text with appropriate forms of the verbs in the box. Then listen and check your answers.

> be   appear   make   never appear
> have   come   take   begin   be   earn

3 Complete the sentences using an appropriate form of the verbs in the box.

> go   eat   lie   meet
> rain   release   work

1 David _____ an apple when he broke a tooth.
2 We were very excited because we _____ to Disneyland before.
3 By lunchtime she was exhausted because she _____ hard all morning.
4 The weather was terrible. In fact, it _____ on the day we arrived and on the day we left!
5 When I opened the fridge, I found that my flatmate _____ all the food!
6 Oliver Stone's film, *Alexander*, _____ in 2005.
7 When she came into the house, Carla's skin was very red – she _____ in the sun all day.
8 My mother _____ my father at a nightclub in 1982.

Vocabulary | time expressions

4 Complete the sentences using words or phrases from the box. One of them is not needed.

> after that   at that time   until   for the previous
> from that point on   since then   throughout
> up until that point   while

1 _____ century, the two countries had been at war.
2 I stopped smoking three years ago and I haven't had a single cigarette _____.
3 He got sick last year but _____ he had been very healthy.
4 Mrs Thatcher was Prime Minister _____ the 1980s.
5 It was the late 1950s and _____ there were almost no supermarkets in England.
6 We missed our connecting flight and _____ things just got worse.
7 Giovanni used to look after the children _____ Clara was at work.
8 The mechanic arrived and repaired our car. _____ we were able to continue on our journey.

Writing

5 Write a short story based on the pictures. Write one or two sentences for each picture using the prompts.

Deborah/love/Tiddles
upset/when /missing
notices/offer/reward

Mr and Mrs
Branksome/enjoy/
watch TV
TV/very old

one evening/
something wrong/
picture
nothing wrong/TV set

take torch/outside
something wrong/
aerial?

see/cat
phone/fire brigade

firefighter/ladder/
rescue

return/cat/Deborah
give/reward

use/money
buy/brand-new
television

Vocabulary | materials

1 Use the clues to complete the crossword.

Across

1 cheap shoes and toys (*n*)
2 antique vases are made from it (*n*)
5 good material for summer clothes (*n*)
7 slightly elastic (*adj*)
9 has a bright surface (*adj*)
10 car tyres (*n*)
11 the opposite of *smooth* (*adj*)
14 perfect for a wedding dress (*n*)

Down

1 comes from trees (*n*)
3 shoes and belts (*n*)
4 opposite of *hard* (*adj*)
6 has an even surface (*adj*)
7 when something gets wet (*adj*)
8 like something animals have to keep them warm (*adj*)
12 a wedding ring (*n*)
13 a strong metal (*n*)

Pronunciation

2 **3.2** Answer the questions. Then listen and check.

1 Which letter isn't pronounced in:
   iron   silver
2 Is the letter 'o' pronounced the same in:
   gold   bronze
3 Is the letter 'c' pronounced the same in:
   cotton   lycra
4 Is the stress on the first or second syllable in:
   rubber   denim

Reading

3 **a** Read the text (don't worry about the gaps). Answer the questions.

1 What are *convenience stores*?
2 What is sometimes surprising about these places?
3 Who usually works in these stores in London?
4 How do these stores find employees?
5 How are family members paid for their work?

b Replace the underlined words and phrases in the following sentences with words and phrases from the text.

1 Harrods is a <u>famous</u> department store in London. _____
2 They've just bought a <u>large</u> house. _____
3 People who live in the country are sometimes prejudiced against <u>people who live in a city</u>. _____
4 We <u>hardly ever</u> take holidays. _____
5 The government is considering changing the law on <u>people moving to this country from another one</u>. _____
6 My parents <u>own and manage</u> a dry cleaning business. _____
7 I have never understood the <u>financial basis</u> of international trade. _____
8 The <u>origin</u> of the River Nile is in Uganda. _____

Asian Shopping

Visitors to London, New York and Los Angeles often remark on how easy it is to buy (1) _____ things at any time of the day or night. It isn't the well-known department stores, large supermarkets or huge shopping malls that they are talking about but those tiny shops (2) _____ Americans call 'convenience stores' and the British call 'corner shops'.

Grammar | articles

4 Complete the numbered gaps in the reading text in Ex. 3 with *a*, *an*, *the* or the zero article (–).

5 Ten of the sentences contain mistakes. Tick (✓) the correct sentences and correct the mistakes in the others.

1 Would you prefer milk or cream in your coffee?
2 Janine and Mike have got beautiful garden.
3 She'd been living in the Los Angeles since the 1980s.
4 Heathrow is the busiest airport in the United Kingdom.
5 When I was young I wanted to be astronaut.
6 Let's have another look at a first one they showed us.
7 I think mobile phone is the greatest invention ever.
8 Teresa's first husband was an engineer.
9 Rudolf's planning to study the philosophy at university.
10 Have you got the double room with a sea view?
11 The Azores are in the middle of Atlantic Ocean.
12 Geography was my favourite subject at school.
13 I love looking at a moon at night.
14 This is most exciting book I've read for a long time.
15 St Moritz is one of the most expensive ski resorts in the Alps.

How to... | communicate interactively

6 Choose the correct alternative.

A: How do you (1) *think/feel* about reality TV shows?
B: You mean things like *Big Brother*?
A: Yes.
B: I think they're quite exciting. What (2) *for/about* you? (3) *How/What* do you think?
A: I think they're awful. They make ordinary people look stupid.
B: Perhaps. But isn't it (4) *real/true* that people choose to be on them? Nobody forces them to take part.
A: I suppose so. But (5) *do/are* you agree that TV companies take advantage of people sometimes?
B: Not really. But I think it's important that the people understand what will happen to them afterwards.
A: Yes. You're right. What (6) *more/else* do you think is important?

They may not always be situated on corners, but they are certainly convenient for tourists and for those city-dwellers who work long hours and don't have time to shop during the day. As people in large cities work longer and longer hours the availability of late-night shopping has become a necessity rather than a luxury.

(3) _____ other thing that sometimes causes surprise is that these shops are rarely owned or staffed by local people. The English-sounding names of 'Super Saver', 'Bargain Supplies' or 'Mini-market' give no clue to the origin of the people working inside the store. In fact, they often seem to be staffed by (4) _____ people from various parts of Asia. Their nationalities often reflect the history of immigration to the country concerned, and they frequently come from nations with a reputation for successful trade and shopkeeping. In New York and Los Angeles it is often Koreans and Chinese who run these stores and in London it is people from the Indian sub-continent.

But what are the economics of such places? How can tiny shops make any profit when employees have to be paid to work (5) _____ such long hours? (6) _____ answer lies partly in the Asian culture of hard work, but is mainly due to the tradition of the extended family. This is very different from the typical Western family in which the individual members have separate lives and careers. When (7) _____ Asian family owns a shop everyone gets involved – brothers, sisters, uncles, aunts, cousins, grandparents and children – everybody is expected to work behind the counter. Thus there is (8) _____ guaranteed source of staff available to work from early morning until late at (9) _____ night. And rather than being paid salaries, the members of the family simply share in (10) _____ profits at the end of the year. It is a recipe that has brought wealth to many immigrant families and made life a lot easier for those of us who run out of milk at eleven o'clock on a Sunday evening!

Reading

1 **a** Read the information about five leading multinational companies and tick (✓) the correct column.

	Nestlé	Coca-Cola	Zara	Shell	Gap
1 the youngest company					
2 the oldest company					
3 has the most shops					
4 has the highest value of sales					
5 based in San Francisco					
6 founded in London					
7 employs the most people					
8 employs the fewest people					
9 famous for its advertisements					
10 owns businesses in 200 countries					

b Find words in the text that mean:

1 drinks (*n*) _____
2 company that makes products (*n*) _____
3 doesn't include alcohol (*adj*) _____
4 started a company or institution (*v*) _____
5 company that takes products to many different locations (*n*) _____
6 famous names or labels belonging to a company (*n*) _____
7 throughout the world (*adj*) _____
8 eat or drink (*v*) _____

Multinational Factfile

Nestlé was founded by Henri Nestlé in 1866. Its headquarters are in Vevey, Switzerland. Nestlé is currently the world's largest manufacturer of food and beverages, with international sales of eighty-seven billion Swiss Francs (sixty-eight billion dollars). Nestle employs 247000 people all over the world.

Coca-Cola is based in Atlanta, Georgia, USA. Founded in 1886, it is now the world's largest manufacturer and distributor of non-alcoholic beverages. Through the 400 businesses it owns in 200 different countries, it employs around one million people. It is estimated that 1.3 billion Coca-Cola drinks are consumed every day. Its sales are worth almost twenty-three billion dollars per year.

Zara is one of Europe's best known brands of clothes stores. It is part of the Inditex group, based in La Coruña, Spain. The first Zara shop opened in La Coruña in 1975. The group now owns 2391 stores in fifty-seven countries. Its sales are 5.7 billion euros (around seven billion dollars) and it employs 47046 people in fifty-seven countries.

Shell is a multinational company famous for its petrol stations and oil production facilities. Founded by Marcus Samuel in London in 1833, the company merged with the Royal Dutch group in 1907. Shell's international headquarters is now in the Hague, Holland. Shell operates in 140 countries and employs around 112000 people. Shell generates sales in the region of eighteen billion dollars from its worldwide operations.

Famous for its clothes stores and imaginative advertising campaigns, Gap is one of the world's most recognisable clothing brands. The first Gap store opened in San Francisco, California, in 1969, and the company is still based in this city. There are now 3000 Gap stores worldwide, employing 150000 people. The company achieves sales of around sixteen billion dollars annually.

Grammar | adjectives and adverbs

2 Rewrite each sentence with the word in brackets in the correct position.

Some of these new computer games are challenging. (incredibly)

Some of these new computer games are incredibly challenging.

1 When I have a headache all I want to do is lie down. (bad)

_____

_____

2 He didn't work so he was bound to fail the exam. (hard)

_____

_____

3 You're very early; did you drive? (fast)

_____

_____

4 Anna is always dressed in designer outfits. (expensively)

_____

_____

5 The clients will expect to get a discount. (certainly)

_____

_____

6 It snowed throughout our holiday. (heavily)

_____

_____

7 He interrupted me in the middle of my speech. (rudely)

_____

_____

8 Do you know them? (well)

_____

_____

9 I'm going to take the First Certificate exam this year. (definitely)

_____

_____

10 The weather can be hot in September. (surprisingly)

_____

_____

3 Match the underlined phrases with words and phrases in the box. Three of the words and phrases are not needed.

> completely ruined   recently   hard   hardly
> high   late   near   nearly   probably
> reasonably priced   unbelievably
> unlikely   well

1 This new computer is <u>not expensive at all</u>. _____

2 Our holiday was <u>totally spoilt</u> by the awful weather. _____

3 She hasn't been coming to lessons <u>in the last few weeks</u>. _____

4 The class found the exercise <u>difficult</u>. _____

5 My uncle speaks Polish <u>fluently</u>. _____

6 We'll <u>almost certainly</u> move to the country next year. _____

7 My son is <u>almost</u> six years old now. _____

8 Jimmy getting a promotion seems <u>rather hard to believe</u>. _____

9 Sheila handed in her essay <u>after it was due</u>. _____

10 The plane flew <u>at a great height</u> over the city. _____

Vocabulary | verb phrases with *take*

4 Choose the correct words to complete the sentences.

1 Nearly all the students ___ the survey.
   A took part of   **B** took in   **C** took part in

2 You should never take good health ___.
   A for grant   **B** as granted   **C** for granted

3 A Korean company has ___ that old factory.
   A taken over   **B** taken up   **C** taken out

4 I tried it for a month but I didn't really ___ that new diet.
   A take to   **B** take at   **C** take in

5 Seeing the sun set over the mountains really took my breath ___.
   A over   **B** out   **C** away

6 He wasn't paying much attention so he didn't take ___.
   A it in all   **B** it all in   **C** it all through

7 It didn't worry me at all, I took ___.
   A it in the stride   **B** all in my stride
   C it all in my stride

8 The use of electric cars has never really ___ in the USA.
   A taken off   **B** taken part in   **C** taken out

Review and consolidation unit 3

Narrative tenses

1 Complete the sentences using the correct form of verbs in the box.

> build   clean   have   invade   play
> start   take   wait   watch   work

1 Millie was covered in dust. She _____ the loft all morning.
2 Napoleon _____ Russia in 1812.
3 I managed to finish my essay while the children _____ in the garden.
4 By the time the train arrived I _____ for more than two hours.
5 I was delayed by the traffic so when I got to the golf course I found my friends _____ without me.
6 The Great Pyramid _____ about 4000 years ago.
7 We _____ television when we heard an enormous bang in the street.
8 By the time I got down to the swimming pool the other guests _____ all the sun beds.
9 When he got home Jack collapsed onto the sofa, exhausted – he _____ at the factory all day.
10 I _____ a bath when I heard the news on the radio.

Vocabulary

2 Match the objects 1–12 with the describing/material words a–l.

1	a wedding ring	a	lycra
2	a mirror	b	silk
3	a pair of swimming trunks	c	rough
		d	denim
4	bed sheets	e	gold
5	ice on a road	f	slippery
6	a cushion	g	stretchy
7	a pair of jeans	h	soft
8	car tyres	i	leather
9	a wedding dress	j	shiny
10	an elastic band	k	rubber
11	a mountain path	l	cotton
12	expensive shoes		

3 Use the clues to complete the crossword.

Across

4 What is the ___ dress of your country?
5 I got a job in March but for the ___ two months I was unemployed.
6 The pyramids are the greatest monuments of ___ Egypt.
8 There was rationing ___ the Second World War.
9 My grandmother is in a home for ___ people.

Down

1 Some of my aunt's clothes are very old-___.
2 Up until that ___ I had been an engineer.
3 ___ clothes aren't always expensive.
6 That old hotel is full of beautiful ___ furniture.
7 What will life be like in the 22nd ___?

Articles

4 Choose the correct alternative.

Isambard Kingdom Brunel

Isambard Kingdom Brunel was (1) *most/the most/a most* famous British engineer of the 19th century.

Born in 1806 in (2) *a Portsmouth/the Porstmouth/Portsmouth*, his first major work was the construction of a railway between London and Bristol in the west of England. The construction of (3) *a railway/the railway/railway* involved building (4) *a tunnel/tunnel/the tunnel* near the town of Box in Somerset. It was three kilometres long, (5) *longest/a longest/the longest* tunnel ever constructed at the time.

After his success with railways, Brunel turned his attention to (6) *the ships/ships*. He wanted to connect his railway line in Bristol with New York in (7) *United States/a United States/the United States*. In 1838 he built the 'Great Western', the first large steam-powered ship, which crossed (8) *the Atlantic/Atlantic/an Atlantic* in only fifteen days.

Brunels' next project was to build (9) *the ship/a ship/ship* made of iron. He achieved this in 1843 with the 'Great Britain'. It was also the first to be driven by (10) *a propeller/the propeller*.

(11) *The ambition/An ambition/Ambition* and (12) *the stubbornness/a stubbornness/stubbornness* were the greatest features of Brunel's character; he always strove to design the biggest and best.

Adjectives and adverbs

5 Eight of the sentences contain mistakes. Find the mistakes and correct them.

1 Heinrich often arrives lately for work.
2 We had to drive slowly because of the heavy rain.
3 I find people around here are general quite friendly.
4 She's much better; she's feeling finely today.
5 My sister can type amazingly quick.
6 Despite studying hardly, Maria failed the test.
7 Have you seen any good films recently?
8 I thought that book was more interestingly than the others.
9 Have you ever noticed how highly frogs can jump?
10 This is definite the best restaurant we've been to for ages.

6 Rewrite the sentences with the words in the correct order.

1 The professor in a friendly way treats all his students.
_____
_____

2 Isabel is the oldest definitely student in our class.
_____
_____

3 I washed this morning the sheets.
_____
_____

4 My brother forgets sometimes his PIN number.
_____
_____

5 Daniela left in the corner of the room her suitcase.
_____
_____

6 The children forgot stupidly to bring their swimming costumes.
_____
_____

7 He wasn't dangerously driving, but he was going quite fast.
_____
_____

8 She has a personality warm and caring.
_____
_____

Vocabulary

7 Choose the correct alternative.

1 Watching the sunset in Hawaii took my breath *out/away*.
2 It's very hard to take *in/out* all this information.
3 Marco's relaxed about what happened; he took it all in his *steps/stride*.
4 Mr Lester is going to take *under/over* the Glasgow branch.
5 Young people often take modern technology completely *for/of* granted.
6 I'm taking part *in/at* a demonstration against the war.
7 Dan took *at/to* his fiancée's parents as soon as he met them.
8 Playing cricket has never really taken *out/off* in Europe.

8 Rewrite the sentences using nouns to replace the phrases in *italics*.

She *writes books for a living*.

She is a writer.

1 Emma *loves being a mother*.
_____

2 *Having friends* is the most important thing for Pepe.
_____

3 David *plays the piano professionally*.
_____

4 We need to increase *the amount we produce*.
_____

5 *Being happy* is more important than wealth.
_____

6 I'm not very pleased with the *thing you arranged*.
_____

7 Professor Grant *invents things*.
_____

8 Children love *feeling excited*.
_____

9 There is a lot of crime in this *place where neighbours live*.
_____

10 My brother *makes a living studying physics*.
_____

Reading

1 **a** Read the newspaper article and choose the best title.

1. Newspapers' Deadly Rival
2. Blogging Websites
3. The Internet News Millionaire

b Read the article again. Mark the sentences true (T) or false (F).

1. Drudge calls himself 'the ultimate blogger'. ☐
2. He loved news and current affairs even as a child. ☐
3. He was a journalist for *The Washington Star*. ☐
4. The Internet didn't exist when Drudge was a child. ☐
5. Drudge got his news from talking to people. ☐
6. He interviewed Monica Lewinsky in 1998. ☐
7. The *Drudge Report* is very useful for people who want up-to-date news. ☐
8. Matt Drudge doesn't think the Internet will take over from newspapers in the future. ☐

c Find the following phrases in the text and match them with the meanings a–j.

1. sprung up (para 1) ☐
2. stems from (para 2) ☐
3. fanatical obsession (para 2) ☐
4. dead-end jobs (para 2) ☐
5. sifting through (para 3) ☐
6. inside stories (para 3) ☐
7. juiciest gossip (para 3) ☐
8. breaking news (para 3) ☐
9. a 'must see' resource (para 4) ☐
10. news junkie (para 4) ☐

a. things that are happening now
b. someone who wants to know the latest news all the time
c. looking very carefully at all the details to find something
d. an overriding interest in something
e. began/originated with
f. a very useful or valuable place to find things
g. information from people who are involved in actual events
h. work that has no future and doesn't lead to a career
i. appeared from nowhere
j. exciting or shocking scandal

1 This is Matt Drudge, millionaire founder and owner of the *Drudge Report*, the first and most successful online 'newspaper'. People have called Drudge the ultimate blogger but he doesn't accept the description. He considers the *Drudge Report* to be a proper newspaper, very different from the thousands of weblogs which have sprung up on the Internet.

2 Drudge's fascination for news and gossip stems from a childhood job delivering papers for *The Washington Star*. It gave him plenty of time and opportunity to catch up with the latest news. Uninterested in school work or sport, Drudge developed a fanatical obsession with rumours and political gossip. At school his only good grades were for current affairs. Following a series of dead-end jobs Drudge ended up in Los Angeles in the 1990s, just in time for the beginning of what was to become the Internet.

3 The fledgling World Wide Web was a fertile hunting ground for Drudge. He spent hours sifting through the newsgroups and rudimentary websites that then existed, searching for rumours and inside stories from the political and entertainment worlds. He launched the *Drudge Report* website in 1995, a daily 'rumour bulletin' containing his version of the latest and juiciest gossip from Hollywood and Washington. Always managing to be the first with breaking news, Drudge's success was assured when he became the first person to publicise the Monica Lewinsky scandal in 1998.

4 Now with a turnover of over $1 million a year and many thousands of subscribers, the *Drudge Report* has become a 'must see' resource for those hungry for the latest news and gossip. But will the ever-increasing availability of news on the Internet mean the end for its older rival, the conventional newspaper? Drudge doesn't think so. He sees the two working together. As far as the news junkie Drudge is concerned there can never be too much news ...

Grammar | *If* structures (1)

2 Rewrite the sentences using conditionals. Start each sentence with *If*. Be careful with modal verbs.

(1st Conditional)

I hope he asks me to marry him because I would accept.

If he asks me to marry him, I'll accept.

1 I'm planning to get a laptop so I can send emails when I'm travelling.

_____

2 I don't want to be late for my interview so I hope the train comes on time.

_____

3 Maribel hopes to pass the driving test because she wants to buy a car.

_____

(2nd Conditional)

The government wants to build more roads but they don't have enough money.

If the government had more money, it would build more roads.

4 I'd like to swim more often but I don't live near a pool.

_____

5 Terry would like to travel around the world but he's scared of flying.

_____

6 Celia's dream is to join a choir but unfortunately she can't sing.

_____

(3rd Conditional)

I met him because I went to the cinema.

If I hadn't gone to the cinema, I wouldn't have met him.

7 Dave won the prize because he knew all the answers.

_____

8 Helena didn't go to the concert because she lost the tickets.

_____

9 Malik might have got a promotion but his sales figures were disappointing.

_____

10 We had to queue up for tickets so we missed the start of the show.

_____

3 Complete the dialogue using appropriate conditional forms of the verbs in brackets.

Ann: Excuse me. I (1) _____ (like) to report a stolen handbag.

Officer: Of course, madam. Let me take some details. Your name?

Ann: Mrs Ann Kendall.

Officer: And where and when did this happen?

Ann: At Denham's department store, about twenty minutes ago. I put my bag down while I was paying at the register ...

Officer: And someone took your bag?

Ann: Exactly. If I'd been paying attention, it (2) _____ (not happen).

Officer: Any idea who did it?

Ann: Not really. If there (3) _____ (be) anyone suspicious, I would have noticed.

Officer: Were there any security cameras there?

Ann: I don't think so. I'm sure they (4) _____ (tell) me if they had had any.

Officer: And what was in the bag?

Ann: Everything. My mobile phone, keys ...

Officer: Any credit cards?

Ann: Yes, one. The thief might try to use it.

Officer: Well, if you (5) _____ (phone) your credit card company now, you (6) _____ (be able) to cancel the cards before anyone can use them.

Ann: OK. But what about my keys? The thief might be able to get into my house.

Officer: Was there anything in your bag that had your address on it, like a driving licence?

Ann: No, I don't think so.

Officer: Well, don't worry. If the thief (7) _____ (not have) your address, he (8) _____ (not know) where you live, will he?

Ann: No, I suppose not. Do you think there's any chance of me getting the bag back?

Officer: It's hard to say, but if anybody (9) _____ (find) the bag, we (10) _____ (contact) you straight away.

Writing

4 Imagine you are a famous person. Write a diary entry or a blog about an exciting day in your life. Write about 100 words. Look at the questions and page 50 of the Students' Book to help you.

- Where were you?/Why were you there?
- What happened?/What time did it happen?
- How do you feel about what happened?

Vocabulary | physical movements

1   Choose the correct alternative.

1   Graham felt very relieved when the plane *leaned/landed* safely on the runway.
2   I'm going to *leap/flip* across the stream. It's only a metre wide.
3   Don't *lean/bend* out of the train window. It's dangerous.
4   You should always *stretch/bend* your knees when lifting heavy objects.
5   A good cure for backache is to lie on your side and *lean/tuck* your knees under your chin.
6   A good sense of *balance/swing* is the secret to riding a bicycle.
7   Katie hit the ball and watched it *roll/flip* along the ground.
8   In the forest the monkeys were *swinging/stretching* from tree to tree.

Writing | explaining how to do something

2   Rewrite the explanation of how to change a flat tyre as instructions. Use imperatives and short sentences. The first two instructions have been done for you.

- *Stop the car.*
- *Put on the handbrake.*

How to change a flat tyre

Getting a puncture in one of your car's tyres can be very annoying, and it's dangerous to attempt to drive a car that has a flat tyre. Luckily, changing the tyre is really quite easy. First of all you should stop the car and make sure the handbrake is on. Then look in the boot of the car and find the spare tyre, take it out and put it on the ground. Then you can take out the jack and the wrench – they're usually kept in a bag somewhere in the car boot.

If your wheel has a cover, you should remove it. Using the wrench, each of the nuts should be loosened slightly (one full turn counter-clockwise). Now you are ready to raise the car off the ground. Carefully position the jack (your car owner's manual will tell you where you need to place it) and gradually raise the car about 10 centimetres off the ground by turning the handle on the jack.

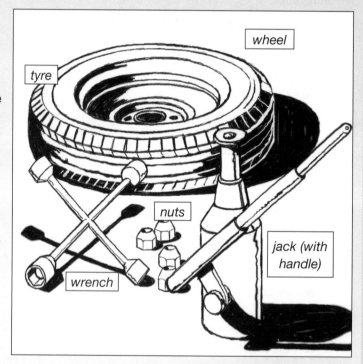

Now you can use the wrench to completely unscrew the nuts on the wheel. After removing the nuts you'll be able to pull the wheel off. Don't forget to put it in the boot so you can take it to be repaired later! Now you should lift up the spare wheel and slip it into position, putting the nuts back and tightening them up by hand – don't use the wrench.

Once you've done that you can lower the car back on to the ground. Now it's time to really tighten the nuts – so use the wrench and turn the nuts clockwise as hard as you can. Replace the wheel cover if you've got one. Make sure you've put the jack, the wrench and the old wheel in the boot and you're ready to go!

Listening and grammar |
expressing obligation

3 a 🔲 **4.1** Cover the tapescript. Listen to the dialogue between Alice and her great grandfather. Answer the questions.

1 What is Alice using?
2 What does her great grandfather do with his hand?
3 Why isn't Alice's photo a success?
4 Why is Alice's great grandfather confused?
5 What was different about taking photos in the 1950s?

b Listen again. Who says it? Write Alice (A) or great grandpa (G).

1 ... you can use your phone. ☐
2 It's got a flash. ☐
3 How do you know ... ? ☐
4 There were plenty of cameras around. ☐
5 ... I like things to be instant ☐

4 Now read the tapescript. Complete the text using the words in the box. Then listen and check.

> needn't   mustn't   don't have to
> should   shouldn't   supposed to be
> don't you have to   had to

5 Read the tapescript again. Find the following words.

1 Two other nouns that mean *photo*.
_____ _____
2 Two verbs that describe a procedure involving chemicals. _____ _____
3 A noun that means *the part of a camera that makes a bright light*.
_____
4 A three-word expression that means *blurred* or *not clear*. _____ _____
_____
5 An adjective that has a similar meaning to *electronic*. _____

TAPESCRIPT

Alice: Come on Great Grandpa, smile. I want to take your photo.

Grandpa: OK Alice, but where's the camera?

Alice: This is a camera.

Grandpa: I thought that was a mobile phone.

Alice: Well yes, but you (1) _____ have a special camera to take photos these days, you can use your phone.

Grandpa: Amazing! (2) _____ I go over to the window where there's more light?

Alice: No, no, you (3) _____ do that. It's got a flash.

Grandpa: Oh, right. Well, I'm ready.

Alice: Umm, you (4) _____ put your hand there. I can't see your face.

Grandpa: Oh. OK.

Alice: Great. Oh, that hasn't come out very well; it's a bit out of focus. I think I'm (5) _____ further away from you.

Grandpa: How do you know it's out of focus? (6) _____ take it for the film to be developed?

Alice: Of course not, it's digital! You can see the picture straight away.

Grandpa: Oh, 'digital', of course. Cameras have certainly changed since I was young!

Alice: In the 1950s? Didn't you have cameras then?

Grandpa: No. There were plenty of cameras around. But you (7) _____ use film and then you had to take it in to a chemist to get it processed and made into prints.

Alice: Boring.

Grandpa: Not really. It was quite exciting waiting for the prints to come back.

Alice: Oh, I couldn't be bothered to wait.

Grandpa: Well, Alice, you (8) _____ be so impatient. Everything comes to those who wait!

Alice: I know, but I like things to be instant. Anyway, let me take another picture of you.

Grandpa: Actually I'm a bit tired now, Alice. Can we do it later?

Alice: Great Grandpa!

6 Six of the sentences contain mistakes. Tick (✓) the correct sentences and correct the mistakes in the others.

1 You're soaking wet. You should have gone out in the rain!
2 We ought to hurry; there isn't much time left.
3 Don't worry. You mustn't pay to get in – it's free.
4 Must you wear a school uniform when you were a child?
5 We really must buy one of those new MP3 players. They're excellent.
6 In Britain you should get a licence to use a TV – it's the law.
7 Excuse me. You needn't smoke in here. It isn't allowed.
8 I'm not surprised you failed the test; you shouldn't have done more work.

Reading

1   **a** Read the advertisement and choose the best answer.

Who is the advertisement mainly aimed at?

1   people who play extreme sports
2   people who might like to try extreme sports
3   people who want to improve their physical fitness

b Read the text again and answer the questions.

1   How many extreme sports are mentioned by name in the text?
2   What two things can you get from the website?
3   Is the weekend suitable for people who aren't physically fit?
4   How many extreme sports were available last year?
5   How much do tickets cost if you buy them at the event itself?

c Find words or phrases in the text that mean:

1   an opportunity to make something imaginary come true (*phrase*)
    _____
2   most important and talented (*adj*)
    _____
3   having a strong desire to do something (*phr v*) _____
4   well protected (*compound adj*)
    _____
5   extremely exciting (*adj*) _____
6   boring, always the same (*adj*)
    _____
7   when you know what will happen in advance (*adj*) _____
8   teachers of physical skills (*n*) _____

How much danger can you take?
Join us for *National Extreme Sports Weekend* and find out!

- Have you ever watched snowboarders and mountain bikers and thought, 'I could do that'?
- Are you tired of the humdrum daily routine and ready to challenge yourself?
- Are you longing for some real risk in your predictable everyday life?

Well, now is your chance to turn fantasy into thrilling reality ...

This year National Extreme Sports Weekend is better than ever. We are offering you the chance to try out over fifty different extreme sports, twice as many as previous years. 100 leading instructors from around the world are waiting to share their top tips and closely-guarded secrets. And you don't even need to be super fit, we have something for everyone!

abseiling   canoeing
    windsurfing
skateboarding   in-line skating
    snowboarding
free running   paragliding

Are you ready for the risk of a lifetime? Are you ready for the challenge?
If you don't come, you'll never know!

National Extreme Sports Weekend is at Fairfield Park, Birmingham 21–22 July.

Tickets and a full schedule of events available from www.NatExsports.com.

£20 on the day, £15 in advance.

Grammar | emphasis

2 Rewrite these sentences using an appropriate form of *do* to make them emphatic.

1 I like your new suit.

_____

2 Amanda complains a lot.

_____

3 He said he was sorry several times.

_____

4 I asked the boss for permission.

_____

5 We know what we are talking about.

_____

3 Choose the correct alternative.

1 I *such/really* didn't understand what she was saying.

2 Their new house was *so/just* expensive.

3 The cotton suit is *much,/such,* much cheaper than the silk one.

4 *Million Dollar Baby* was *such/so* a good film

5 It's a *such,/very,* very good hotel.

6 Clint Eastwood is *such/just* fantastic in that role.

7 His sister is *so/such* beautiful, don't you agree?

8 This new artist is *very,/really,* really talented.

4 Rewrite the sentences to emphasise the <u>underlined</u> word or phrase. Begin each sentence with *It.*

I can't stand <u>her new boyfriend</u>.

It's her new boyfriend that I can't stand.

1 They love <u>Chinese food</u>.

_____

2 She spoke to <u>his assistant</u>.

_____

3 I didn't like <u>the first film</u>.

_____

4 <u>My thumb hurts</u>, not my finger.

_____

5 Clara really doesn't like <u>modern poetry</u>.

_____

6 I really don't understand <u>his attitude</u>.

_____

Pronunciation

5 `4.2` <u>Underline</u> the word which has the strongest stress in these sentences. Then listen and check.

1 No, it was yesterday that I went there.

2 It's the black one that we need.

3 It's the hall that he wants you to decorate.

4 No, it's my left hand that's hurting.

5 It was Jane that wanted to see you.

Vocabulary | phrasal verbs with *out*

6 a Choose the correct alternative.

1 I wasn't able to *find/give* out what time the film starts.

2 You'll have to use another printer. This one's *run/sorted* out of ink.

3 It was hard work but it *fell/turned* out alright in the end.

4 Mel, please *give/take* out a copy to everyone in class 3C.

5 Jim's going to *sort/find* out the files.

b Four of the sentences contain mistakes. Tick (✓) the correct sentences and correct the mistakes in the others.

1 We weren't sure about the babysitter but she took out to be really good.

2 Dan's had to go to the gym on his own since he fell out with his gym partner.

3 My car broke down last week and the mechanic wasn't able to put it out.

4 I'm afraid we only give out catalogues to established clients.

5 Make sure you fall out your cigarettes before you enter the building.

6 If I have a problem with my house, my neighbour turns it out – he's a builder.

How to ... | compare photos

7 Compare and contrast the two photos. Write about 150 words. Make sure you mention the following things.

• two things that are the same

• two things that are different

• speculations about the situations

• your own reactions and opinions

Vocabulary

1 Complete the sentences with words from the box. Two of the words are not needed.

> ambition   substantial   incredibly
> gamble   hardly   luck   vast   endurance
> dream   opportunity

1 She can't run fast but she has a lot of _____ – she can keep running for hours.
2 To be successful in business you need a lot of _____.
3 Although I knew it was a _____, I invested all my money in my best friend's new shop.
4 I'm sorry you didn't win. I hope you have better _____ next time.
5 When I was a child it was my _____ to become an astronaut.
6 Our company made a lot of money this year so we're expecting a _____ pay rise.
7 You should never swim during a thunderstorm; it's _____ dangerous.
8 I'm very glad that I had the _____ to travel when I was young.

If structures (1)

2 Choose the correct form of the verbs to complete the sentences.

1 If Steven hadn't passed the exam, he ___ to university.
   A didn't go   B wouldn't go
   C wouldn't have gone
2 If you ___ some ice in a drink, it makes it cooler.
   A have put   B put   C will put
3 I ___ for the cinema if you pay for the restaurant.
   A paid   B 'll pay   C am paying
4 If you ___ a positive attitude, you won't succeed in business.
   A don't' have   B didn't have   C haven't had
5 What ___ if your car broke down on the motorway?
   A will you do   B would you do
   C are you doing
6 I ___ by taxi if I were you.
   A 'd go   B must go   C will go
7 If John got a pay rise, we ___ to a bigger apartment.
   A might have moved   B might be moving
   C might move
8 They ___ that hotel if they'd known how expensive it was.
   A didn't choose   B wouldn't have chosen
   C wouldn't choose

Vocabulary

3 Match the pictures with the words in the box.

> balance   bend   land   lean
> roll   stretch   swing   tuck

1 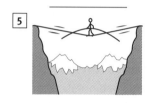	2 
_____	_____
3 	4 
_____	_____
5 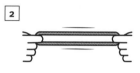	6 
_____	_____
7 	8 
_____	_____

Expressing obligation

4 Choose the correct alternative.

1 In Australia you *have/need* to drive on the left, that's the law.
2 You *mustn't/needn't* use mobile phones while a plane is taking off or landing.
3 You're covered in mud. You *shouldn't/mustn't* have been playing in the garden!
4 I *was supposed to/must* be there by six but I missed my bus.
5 She's been so helpful. Do you think I *have to/ought to* take her a bunch of flowers?
6 Don't worry; we *mustn't/don't have* to stay very long.
7 We *didn't have to/should have* asked for permission before we borrowed her keys.
8 I feel very guilty – perhaps I *ought to/must* apologise to him.
9 The doctor is very busy so you *mustn't/don't have to* be late for the appointment.
10 You *mustn't/needn't* have brought soap; the hotel supplies it free of charge.

Emphasis

5 Put the words in the correct order to make emphatic sentences.

that / the children / go there / It / want to / is

It is the children that want to go there.

1 made me / It was / feel sick / that / the shellfish

_____

_____

2 try / She / you / did / to contact

_____

_____

3 really, / do voluntary work / I / who /really / admire people

_____

_____

4 I / It / my / injured / is / left leg / that

_____

_____

5 such a / footballer / Gerald / good / is

_____

_____

6 money / give / Henrietta / a lot of / to charity / does

_____

_____

7 that / It / mobile phone / was stolen / was / my

_____

_____

8 expensive / very, / My / was / new computer / very

_____

_____

9 do / Javier / did / work / a lot of / for us

_____

_____

10 does / the housework / It / his wife / is / that / most of

_____

_____

6 Complete the sentences with words from the box.

> is   so   that   such   does   did   really   it

1 It is John's children _____ I feel sorry for.

2 I think Sylvia really _____ love him.

3 That flat screen television is _____ expensive.

4 _____ was Elizabeth that I was trying to contact.

5 I _____ try to get front row seats but they were sold out.

6 Monet's paintings are really, _____ beautiful.

7 Clare is _____ a wonderful mother.

8 It _____ the final episode I want you to record.

Vocabulary

7 Complete the sentences with suitable phrasal verbs with *out*.

1 Karl goes to the gym every day and _____ .

2 Although the heat was intense, the firefighters managed to _____ the fire.

3 Excuse me, Alex. Could you _____ the time of the next train to Exeter?

4 Can you get me a few things at the shops? We've _____ of bread, coffee and milk.

5 Don't worry about tidying up – I'll help you _____ the mess.

6 We were good friends for years then suddenly, for no reason, we _____ .

7 While we were waiting the secretary _____ some magazines for us to read.

8 I thought the car had broken down but in fact it _____ that we had just run out of petrol!

8 Use the clues to complete the crossword.

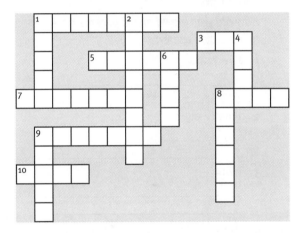

Across

1 The curtains don't quite touch the ground; we need to ___ them by about ten cm.

3 Temperatures can be quite ___ in winter.

5 My husband's very tall so we're increasing the ___ of the doors in our house.

7 He needs a large jacket because of the ___ of his shoulders.

8 Don't disturb her; she's ___ in thought.

9 The government is going to ___ the motorway from three lanes to four.

10 I don't mind short flights but I hate ___ ones.

Down

1 I wish the government would ___ taxes.

2 They are going to ___ the bridge so that large trucks can pass underneath.

4 How ___ is the gate? Will the car get through?

6 How ___ in Mount Everest?

8 Reading this book will increase and ____ your understanding of philosophy.

9 My boss is quite ____-minded.

Listening

1   a   **5.1**   Cover the tapescript. Listen to an American radio interview. Complete the notes in the table.

Work	US: *Joe makes feature films.*
	UK: (1) _____
Film-making	US: (2) _____
	UK: (3) _____
Shopping	US: (4) _____
	UK: (5) _____
Weather	US: (6) _____
	UK: *It was always cloudy.*

b   Listen again and write the questions for the following answers.

about ten

How old was Joe when his parents gave him a movie camera?

1   five years

_____

_____

2   twenty-eight

_____

_____

3   work

_____

_____

4   three

_____

_____

5   There is more money involved.

_____

_____

6   walking to the shops

_____

_____

7   Because of the enormous distances between places.

_____

_____

8   Because it was always so cloudy.

_____

_____

c   Now read the tapescript. Find short phrases (not single words) that mean:

1   when people from many backgrounds mix together _____

2   managers of film companies _____

3   do something that irritates people _____

4   constantly supervising and watching somebody _____

5   making films in real places, not in studios _____

TAPESCRIPT

I: Hi everybody and welcome once again to *America – the Melting Pot*. This week we have as our guest the British film director, Joe Grendal. Welcome to the show, Joe.

J: Thanks. It's great to be here.

I: Now, you've been in the US for the last five years. Is that right?

J: Yeah. I came here when I was twenty-eight.

I: What made you choose to live in the States?

J: Well, work really. I had a reasonably successful career back in London, making TV commercials and short films, but I really wanted to get into feature films.

I: You made those famous commercials for trainers, didn't you?

J: Yes. I (1) _____ do lots of work for sportswear companies. Some of the commercials I made were shown in the States and that's really how the connection with Hollywood began. Some American studio executives saw my work on TV here and invited me over.

I: Were you always interested in movie-making?

J: I guess so. Certainly when I was a child I (2) _____ spend hours watching Hollywood movies on TV and my parents gave me a movie camera when I was about ten. I (3) _____ drive the family mad rushing around filming everything!

I: You've made three films over here now. How does film-making here compare to Britain?

J: It's not that different, really. But there's a lot more money involved. Back in the UK we (4) _____ have much contact with the accountants. But here they're on top of you all the time!

I: Do you find that difficult?

J: Well, let's just say I'm still (5) _____ it!

I: Is there anything you really miss from the old country?

J: For me, no. But my wife misses walking to the shops. The distances between places are so enormous here, so you have to drive everywhere. In London we had lots of local shops so we (6) _____ usually walk to get our shopping.

I: Yes. Nobody walks here. They go to the gym instead!

J: I know. People drive to the gym and then spend hours walking on the treadmills. Crazy!

I: Right! Er, the weather, surely that's very different here?

J: Sure. I love the sunny weather here in southern California. In fact, it means we can do a lot of location work. That's something new for me because it was always so cloudy in England we (7) _____ do much outdoors – I always preferred to be inside a nice warm studio!

I: What about the way we talk – the American accent ...

J: Oh, I (8) _____ that. It's probably more difficult for you lot to understand me. Although I can't say I've really had any problems.

Grammar | *used to/get used to/would*

2 Look at the tapescript for Ex. 1 again. Complete the text using appropriate forms of *used to*, *get used to* or *would*. Then listen and check.

3 Tick (✓) the forms which are possible in each sentence and put a cross (✗) by the ones which are not possible. More than one form may be possible.

1 When I was a child I ___ play football all the time.
 A would ☐ B got used to ☐ C used to ☐

2 Gerald ___ be overweight.
 A used to ☐ B would ☐ C didn't use to ☐

3 We ___ go to bed early when we were small.
 A didn't use to ☐ B would ☐ C used to ☐

4 It took me ages to ___ this new diet.
 A get use to ☐ B get used to ☐ C getting used to ☐

5 ___ that new computer?
 A Are you getting used to ☐ B Do you get used to ☐
 C Are you used to ☐

6 ___ be in the school swimming team?
 A Are they used to ☐ B Did they use to ☐
 C Didn't they use to ☐

7 Do you think she ___ living on her own?
 A gets used to ☐ B will get used to ☐ C is used to ☐

8 Our youngest child ___ watch television for hours on end.
 A would ☐ B used to ☐ C was used to ☐

9 ___ live in the countryside before you came here?
 A Do you get used to ☐ B Did you use to ☐
 C Would you ☐

10 ___ driving on the right?
 A Do you used to ☐ B Are you getting used to ☐
 C Are you use to ☐

Vocabulary | appearance

4 Use the clues to complete the crossword with words to describe appearance.

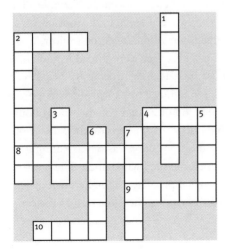

Across
2 like the sea
4 top models are like this
8 graceful and attractive
9 a type of hair, but not straight
10 no hair

Down
1 Arnold Schwarzenegger
2 old people have these on their faces
3 not a natural hair colour
5 light brown
6 you're like this if you sunbathe
7 not slim, not fat, not tall

Writing

5 a Look at the photos and write notes in the table.

Jennifer

Harry

	Jennifer	Harry
Age		
Face		
Hair		
Build		
Clothes		

b Use the information to write a short description of each person.

Reading

1 **a** Read the short story quickly and choose the best title.

1 The Swiss Burglar

2 Driving in Milan

3 The Disastrous Holiday

Kirsten and Dieter were very excited about their driving holiday in Italy. They packed their convertible Mercedes with three suitcases and set off from their home in Zürich early in the
5 morning. The weather was warm and, as they drove across the Swiss border into Italy, they lowered the roof and enjoyed the pleasant sensation of the warm spring air rushing past their heads.

By the middle of the afternoon they had reached
10 Milan. Kirsten (1) _____ map-reading but she was sure they (2) _____ make their way to the centre of the city, find a parking space and enjoy a delicious late lunch at a local restaurant. As they drove into one of the city's quiet suburbs
15 they suddenly heard a loud bang and felt something crash into the back of their Mercedes. Turning around they saw a small motorbike lying on its side behind their car with two young men sprawled on the road beside it. Dieter stopped the car and
20 jumped out to see if he (3) _____ help. One of the young men was groaning loudly. Kirsten (4) _____ give first aid so she opened her door and approached the groaning man. Suddenly the two men jumped up and rushed towards the
25 Mercedes. In less than two seconds they had leapt into the car and driven off at high speed, leaving Dieter and Kirsten standing in the street.

Dieter started shouting for help in German. But there was nobody around to hear him. At first
30 Kirsten wasn't too worried. She (5) _____ speak Italian either, but she was sure they'd (6) _____ find a police station nearby. After half an hour of walking they had still failed to find a police officer or anyone to help them and they
35 began to get more worried. Their passports, credit cards, mobile phones and money had all been in the car and Dieter was worried that the thieves might be using his credit cards to go on a massive spending spree.

40 About twenty minutes later they saw a police car driving along the street and they rushed into the road to flag it down. Dieter tried to explain what had happened to the police officer. But the officer (7) _____ understand German and decided
45 to take the two Swiss tourists back to the police station. He was sure one of his colleagues would (8) _____ translate for them. Unfortunately as he was driving back to the police station there was an emergency call on his radio and he
50 was instructed to drive to the scene of a serious accident. Dieter and Kirsten were forced to sit in the back of the police car for another two hours while the officer dealt with the emergency.

By the time they arrived at the local police station
55 it was eight o'clock in the evening and they were exhausted. Using the police station's phone, Dieter (9) _____ contacting his credit card company to cancel his cards. Once they'd done this they decided the best thing was to get home as quickly as
60 possible. A police officer drove them to the railway station and lent them the money to buy two tickets. They just (10) _____ catch the last train – the slow overnight service back to Zürich.

Relieved to be on their way home, the couple soon
65 fell asleep. They woke at seven in the morning as the train pulled into Zürich's central station. With no money for a taxi, they were forced to walk back to their house. Just as they turned into their street they saw a large removal truck leaving. Kirsten was
70 surprised; she didn't think any of their neighbours were moving house. As they approached their house they noticed the front door was open. Running into the house, Dieter gasped with shock. The house was completely empty. Then he remembered. Their
75 house keys had been on the same ring as the car key …

b Read the text again and number the events 1–12 in the correct order.

- [ ] Two Italian men drive off in their Mercedes.
- [ ] They have to wait while the police officer deals with an accident.
- [ ] They catch the slow train back to Zürich.
- [1] Dieter and Kirsten leave Zürich.
- [ ] They get into an Italian police car.
- [ ] Dieter and Kirsten get back to their house in Zürich.
- [ ] They get out of their car to see what has happened.
- [ ] The Italian men steal everything from their house and drive away in a van.
- [ ] They walk around trying to find a police station.
- [ ] The police take Dieter and Kirsten to the railway station.
- [ ] They drive into the suburbs of Milan.
- [ ] A motorbike crashes into the back of their car.

c Find words and phrases in the text that mean:

1 a car with an opening roof (*adj/n*) _____

2 left on a journey (*phr v*) _____

3 moving quickly (*v*) _____

4 lying with the legs and arms spread out (*v*) _____

5 making noises as if in pain (*v*) _____

6 spending a large amount of money at one time (*phrase*) _____

7 signal a car or taxi to stop (*phr v*) _____

8 very tired (*adj*) _____

9 gave something to somebody but they have to repay it later (*v*) _____

10 a large vehicle used to move furniture (*n*) _____

Grammar | expressing ability

2 Complete the text in Ex. 1 using the words in the box.

> be able to could (x2) couldn't (x2)
> knew how to   manage to
> managed to   succeeded in
> wasn't very good at

3 Complete the sentences using one word only.

1 I'm afraid we weren't _____ to get you any tickets.

2 Did you _____ in getting a pay rise?

3 If they get here on time, they'll _____ able to see the fireworks.

4 I'm terrible _____ cooking so I eat out most nights.

5 _____ you ride a bicycle when you were a child?

6 Clara's really _____ at languages; she speaks three or four fluently.

7 My uncle _____ to get me a job in his office last summer.

8 Excuse me. Do you know _____ to open this window?

9 At the end of the course you _____ be able to take the diploma exam.

10 Don't ask Jane to navigate – she's _____ at map reading.

How to ... | talk about memories

4 Look at the photograph and read the text. There are four factual errors in the text. Find the mistakes and correct them.

This photo really brings back memories of my childhood holidays. We used to go to the seaside in the winter. Although the weather was often too hot, I remember that we always had a lot of fun. We would spend hours swimming in the sea and playing games on the beach. I loved building sand castles and my sisters used to bury my legs in the sand! We spent most of the time laughing and playing tricks on each other. My parents loved driving along the coast, stopping to have picnics in the forest. I would sit on the grass with my three sisters and my mother. My father would serve us drinks and food from a picnic basket. Everything got covered in sand but it still tasted delicious! Yes, I often get nostalgic for those days when I see photos of the seaside.

Vocabulary | feelings

1 Match the statements with the adjectives in the box.

> annoyed   confused   curious
> excited   relieved   sceptical
> shocked   suspicious

1 Thank goodness you're safe. I was so worried about you! _____

2 I wonder what's in that box? I'd love to have a look inside. _____

3 What on earth are we supposed to do? I really can't understand these instructions. _____

4 Wow! Front row seats for the concert! I can't wait! _____

5 His behaviour really gets on my nerves. He's so rude! _____

6 I don't trust our new boss. I'm sure he wants to get rid of me. _____

7 You spent over i500 on a single pair of shoes? That's outrageous! _____

8 The doctor said I should lose weight but most doctors don't know what they're talking about. _____

2 Choose the correct alternative.

1 Sarah doesn't like football or tennis; in fact, she's pretty *uninterested/ uneasy* in sports in general.

2 The children got very *excited/curious* when I told them we were going to Disneyland next summer.

3 I'll get a good grade; I'm always *optimistic/sceptical* about tests.

4 Clive's very *relieved/uneasy* about making the presentation – the idea of standing up in front of a group of people always worries him.

5 They're quite *uninterested/suspicious* about their new neighbour. He seems to do a lot of strange things in the middle of the night.

6 We were very *relieved/uneasy* when we heard that nobody had been hurt in the car crash.

Reading

3 **a** Read the newspaper article. Complete the text with the extracts A–H. Two of the extracts are not needed.

The Musician with no Memory

Police in Sheerness, Kent have appealed for help in identifying a mystery man who was found wandering on a beach two days ago.

The mystery man seems unable to speak or write and may not even understand English. When he was picked up by the police he was smartly dressed in a suit and tie, (1) [_____] It had been raining and his clothes were soaking wet. (2) [_____] He is white and in his twenties or early thirties.

(3) [_____] and put under the supervision of Michael Camp, a local social worker. The mystery deepened when nurses at the hospital gave the man a pen and paper and, (4) [_____], he drew a picture of a grand piano. There is a piano in the hospital's chapel and Mr Camp took the man there. (5) [_____] Onlookers described his performance as 'virtuoso'. Staff at the hospital dubbed him 'The Piano Man'.

Kent Police believe the man may be a professional musician who is suffering from amnesia after some kind of traumatic accident. (6) [_____]. Photos and a description of the man have been circulated around Europe's police forces.

Anyone who thinks they may be able to identify this man is asked to get in touch with the National Missing Persons Helpline.

A The man was taken to Medway Maritime Hospital

B Others think he may be a con artist or an illegal immigrant from Eastern Europe.

C The man was taken to the local hospital, however.

D He proceeded to sit down and play classical music for two hours non-stop.

E rather than writing his name and address

F but the labels were missing and he had no documents on him.

G Nevertheless he is probably not British.

H Although he did not have any obvious injuries the man seemed confused and disoriented.

b Complete the sentences using the prompts in brackets and information from the text.

1 He was _____ but his clothes _____. (dressed/soaking wet)

2 Although he _____, the missing man _____ (speak/play piano)

3 He was _____. However, the _____ (suit/labels)

4 He had no _____. Nevertheless, he _____. (injuries/confused)

5 Though he can't _____, he _____. (words/pictures)

6 He may _____. However, the police _____. (illegal immigrant/musician)

c Find the following words and phrases in the text/extracts and match them with the meanings a–j.

1 appealed ☐
2 wandering ☐
3 disoriented ☐
4 chapel ☐
5 non-stop ☐
6 dubbed ☐
7 virtuoso ☐
8 amnesia ☐
9 traumatic ☐
10 con artist ☐

a gave someone a special name
b someone who makes money from tricking people
c an illness in which you lose your memory
d asked for assistance
e extremely stressful
f confused about where you are/what you are doing
g continuously
h walking around without a purpose
i showing the highest level of skill and talent
j a room for religious ceremonies

Pronunciation

4 **5.2** How do we pronounce the -ed endings of the following adjectives? Tick (✓) the correct column.
Then listen and check.

		/ɪd/	/d/	/t/
1	annoyed			
2	confused			
3	excited			
4	relieved			
5	shocked			
6	uninterested			

Grammar | although/but/however/ nevertheless

5 Complete the sentences using a linking word from the box. Use each linking word once only.

Lizzie has a lot of money. She lives in a small flat.
Although Lizzie has a lot of money, she lives in a small flat.

even though   however   nevertheless   but   although

1 I love vegetables _____ I hate fruit.
2 Your bank account is in credit. _____, we are unable to authorise the loan.
3 _____ there was a lot of rain, a lot of the plants died.
4 We spent two hours at the museum. _____, we forgot to look at the impressionist paintings.
5 He's going bald, _____ he's only nineteen.

6 Each sentence has a mistake with punctuation and/or word order. Rewrite the sentences correctly.

1 The children we met were healthy. But, very badly educated.

2 I've been to New York although, I've never seen the Statue of Liberty.

3 Your visa has expired, nevertheless. We are prepared to allow you to stay for a further three months.

4 I hear Austria is great for skiing holidays though. I've never been there myself.

5 I've lived even though in London for four years, I still get lost on the underground system.

6 My grandparents were poor, but, happy.

7 Although we enjoy long walks. We do find them quite tiring.

8 Pets are not usually permitted in the hotel however. In this case we can make an exception.

Vocabulary

1 Choose the correct words to complete the text.

1 As he gets older, he's getting more and more _____.
   It's so sad.

   A forgetable   B forgetful   C forgetting

2 I get really _____ when I look at these old photos.

   A nostalgic   B remembering   C nostalgia

3 _____ me, what was the name of your first boyfriend?

   A Remember   B Remind   C Reminisce

4 Do you _____ when we used to go to the beach?

   A remind   B memory   C remember

5 My grandparents love to _____ about the old days.

   A reminisce   B nostalgic   C remind

6 The fantastic atmosphere made the trip really _____.

   A memory   B memorable   C nostalgia

used to/get used to/would

2 Rewrite the sentences using the words in brackets.

He doesn't swim in the sea any more. (used)

He used to swim in the sea.

1 Are you becoming accustomed to life in the big city? (getting)

   _____

2 Sally didn't have any friends when she was a child. (use)

   _____

3 I went to the library every morning when I was a student. (would)

   _____

4 The company doesn't export cars to Asia any longer. (used)

   _____

5 Did he become familiar with the software fairly quickly? (get)

   _____

6 When I was young I didn't watch much television. (use)

   _____

7 How often did you get the bus to school? (would)

   _____

8 I've become accustomed to staying up late. (got)

   _____

9 It was easy to become familiar with the new computer. (used)

   _____

10 Pepe lives in a big house now. (didn't)

   _____

Vocabulary

3 Replace the words in brackets with a suitable word to complete the sentences.

1 Derek is _____ (he doesn't have a beard) and has dark blond hair.

2 Mrs Arkwright is eighty-five and her face is covered in _____ (lines).

3 When he was young Jason had a full head of hair but now I'm afraid he's _____ (got no hair on his head).

4 Although her parents have straight hair, Jo's hair is rather _____ (shaped like the letter 'S').

5 My brother started doing bodybuilding a few years ago and now he's very _____ (has lots of muscles).

6 Even when he wears suits Henry manages to look quite _____ (untidy).

7 Everyone in my family has _____ (light brown) hair.

8 To be successful in Hollywood you usually have to be _____ (handsome or pretty).

9 I thought Daniela's hair was naturally blonde but in fact it's _____ (artificially coloured).

10 She has a small _____ (shaped like the letter 'O') face and thick dark hair.

Expressing ability

4 Complete the sentences using expressions of ability and the verbs in brackets.

Jane _____ (not eat or drink) for two hours after the operation.

Jane *won't be able to eat or drink* for two hours after the operation.

1 David _____ (repair) his computer after he had spoken to the technician.

2 When I was a young child I _____ (play) football for hours without getting tired.

3 The children _____ (not come) on holiday with us next summer.

4 My husband is really _____ (cook) but he's hopeless at cleaning.

5 _____ (you/find) their website on the Internet yesterday?

6 By the end of the course you _____ (type) thirty words a minute.

Vocabulary

5 Use the clues to complete the crossword with adjectives.

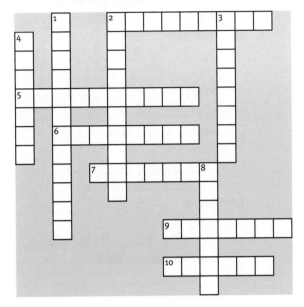

Across

2 when you're not sure you believe that something is true

5 the opposite of *pessimistic*

6 when something you were worried about turns out to be OK

7 when you want to find out what's happening and why

9 the way children feel before a holiday or birthday

10 slightly worried, not relaxed

Down

1 the opposite of *interested*

2 when you think somebody is hiding something bad

3 not certain, not sure, not clear

4 angry

8 when you see or hear something you weren't expecting or prepared for

although/but/however/nevertheless

6 Choose the best way to continue each sentence.

1 Although she had flown many times,
   A Lucy flew quite often.
   B Lucy was still scared of flying.

2 You failed to pass the entrance test.
   A Nevertheless, we are prepared to offer you a place on the course.
   B Even though we are prepared to offer you a place on the course.

3 I wanted to buy a new laptop
   A but all the models I looked at were too expensive.
   B nevertheless all the models were too expensive.

4 The shop wouldn't give us a refund,
   A although they didn't agree to pay for repairs.
   B although they did agree to pay for repairs.

5 Even though I found him boring,
   A I tried to make conversation with him.
   B I didn't bother to make conversation with him.

6 Buying first class tickets was more expensive.
   A However, we thought it was worth it.
   B But we thought it was worth it.

7 Teresa decided to go to work,
   A however she had a headache.
   B even though she had a headache.

8 We realise that the parcel was in good condition when you sent it.
   A Nevertheless, it was damaged when it arrived.
   B Even though it was damaged when it arrived.

Vocabulary

7 Six of the sentences contain mistakes. Find the mistakes and correct them.

1 Alison can be very irritating; she's a real pain of the neck.

2 Joe may be a bit boring but his heart is in the right position.

3 He doesn't find it easy to make friends; in fact, he's rather a cold fish.

4 Karen often says things that hurt people but she doesn't care – she's as hard as a nail.

5 Mike is such a know-everything; he always thinks he knows the answer to every question.

6 When I was young I was a bit of a loner; I didn't have many friends.

7 My colleague's not very ambitious and she certainly isn't a high-flying.

8 Kurt can be such an awkward custom, he's always creating problems for us.

Reading

1 **a** Read the newspaper article quickly and choose the best title.

1 Chinese Motorways

2 Speed Tourists

3 Europe's New Destination

(1) For years tourists (1) _____ to Europe to enjoy its many attractions. From the beaches of the Mediterranean to the castles of Scotland, Europe has something for every kind of holidaymaker to enjoy. Now travel agents (2) _____ a new and rather unexpected attraction to the list – the German motorway system. For the last three years travel companies (3) _____ Chinese tourists to Germany to experience the thrill of driving on its 'autobahns'. This year more than 120000 are expected to arrive.

(2) What is it about Germany's autobahns that tempts tourists to travel from halfway across the world? The answer is simple – speed. More than 8000 kilometres of German motorways have no speed limit – something which is virtually unique in the modern world. Few Europeans realise that Germany's superb roads have an almost mythical reputation in Asia, where highways are often overcrowded, poorly maintained and full of potholes.

(3) Tour operators (4) _____ that offering a Mercedes, Audi or BMW capable of 240 kilometres per hour to holidaymakers is the best way of bringing in much-needed foreign exchange.

For the last few years the Chinese economy (5) _____ rapidly and as a result there are plenty of Chinese travellers wealthy enough to afford the €3000 charged for a six-day 'autobahn tour'. The prices they are charging may seem high, but the 'speed tourists' claim that the thrill of driving at speeds which would almost certainly lead to prison sentences back at home far outweighs the expense involved.

(4) But this new form of tourism (6) _____ so popular with the locals. German road safety groups (7) _____ negatively to the arrival of the Chinese speed tourists. Figures published by the World Health Organisation show that more than 600 people die on China's roads every day. Even taking into consideration the huge population of China, this is still a horrifying statistic. But the Chinese drivers are undeterred, pointing out that since they first started coming three years ago there (8) _____ no major accidents involving speed tourists.

b Read the text again. Write the questions for these answers.

1 three years

_____

_____

2 120000

_____

_____

3 speed

_____

_____

4 8000

_____

_____

5 Mercedes, Audi or BMW

_____

_____

6 240

_____

_____

7 €3000

_____

_____

8 600

_____

_____

c Find these words or phrases in the text.

1 two more nouns that mean *tourists*

_____ _____

2 three more nouns that mean *roads*

_____ _____ _____

3 another expression that means *travel companies*

_____

4 an adverb that means *almost*

_____

5 an adjective that means *like something from a story or legend*

_____

6 an -*ed* adjective that means the opposite of *put off/discouraged*

_____

Grammar | Present Perfect Simple and Continuous

2 Complete the newspaper article in Ex. 1 using Present Perfect Simple or Continuous forms of the verbs in the box. You may need to use negative or passive forms.

> add be bring discover expand flock prove react

3 Write responses using the prompts and appropriate forms of the Present Perfect Simple or Continuous. Add any other words that are necessary.

Why are you so red?

I/lie/sun/all morning

I've been lying in the sun all morning.

1 Can we go back to the car now?
no/I/not pay/shopping/yet

_____

2 Why are the children soaking wet?
they/swim/the lake

_____

3 Have you tried that new French restaurant yet?
no/never/go/there

_____

4 Michael looks tanned.
yes/he/just/come back/Miami Beach

_____

5 Why aren't you having any pudding?
I/follow/strict diet/for/last two months

_____

6 Shall I feed the cats?
no/I/already/do/it

_____

7 Is Maria still working on that report?
yes/she/type/lunchtime

_____

8 You're a good teacher and you seem very experienced.
yes/teach/karate/more than/ten years

_____

9 You look exhausted.
I/wash/the floors/all afternoon

_____

10 Do you still go to the tennis club?
no/I/not be/member/2004

_____

Vocabulary | adjectives with *-ed/-ing* endings

4 Complete the summaries using suitable *-ed* or *-ing* adjectives from the list on page 87 of the Students' Book.

1 **Miranda:** Daniel's behaviour made me very angry.
Miranda feels _____.
Daniel's behaviour was _____.

2 **David:** After listening to her speech, I decided to become a doctor.
Her speech was _____.
David felt _____ by the speech.

3 **Mary:** I thought the exhibition was incredibly interesting.
The exhibition was _____.
Mary was _____ by the exhibition.

4 **José:** That was the scariest film I've ever seen. I've never been so scared!
José was _____ by the film.
The film was _____.

5 **Eloise:** I know the job is quite difficult, but that hasn't put me off doing it.
Eloise doesn't think the job is _____.
She isn't _____ by the job.

Writing

5 You are about to finish a three-month holiday in Kenya. As part of the holiday you have been helping a charity project which teaches English to young children. Complete this email to your friend Sara. Follow this paragraph plan and look at page 162 of the Students' Book to help you.

Paragraph 1

where you are/why you are there/how you feel about it

Paragraph 2

what you do in the morning/in the afternoon/in your free time

Paragraph 3

how you feel about the experience/how feel about finishing and coming home

Hi Sara
I'm having an amazing experience here! I'm

Reading

1 a Read the web page quickly and match the headings A–G with the paragraphs 1–5. Two headings are not needed.

- A Facilities ☐
- B Reservations ☐
- C Location ☐
- D Lapland ☐
- E History ☐
- F The Ice Hotel ☐
- G Construction ☐

b Read the web page again and decide if the statements are true (T) or false (F).

1 The Ice Hotel isn't the sort of building people expect to find in a northern country. ☐
2 People in Jukkasjärvi don't speak Swedish. ☐
3 It takes two days to build the hotel. ☐
4 The hotel is mainly built of ice. ☐
5 A French artist built the first Ice Hotel. ☐
6 Guests sometimes worry about the cold temperatures. ☐
7 Guests can watch films. ☐
8 Visitors can hunt reindeer in the daytime. ☐

c We often use particular adverb and adjective combinations, e.g. *heavily insulated* (paragraph 1). Find five more examples of this type of collocation in the text.

File   Edit   View   History   Bookmark   help   — ✕

Unusual Destinations – number 22

(1) People often choose to have holidays in strange and unusual places. But there can be few places stranger than the Ice Hotel in Sweden, which is visited by almost 37000 people each winter. Built entirely of snow and ice, the hotel is the very opposite of the heavily insulated, centrally heated buildings we normally associate with northern countries. Rather than insulate itself from the cold subzero environment all around it, the hotel embraces the wintry surroundings and makes them into part of its attraction.

(2) The Ice Hotel is situated in the small village of Jukkasjärvi, next to the river Tornealven. Jukkasjärvi lies 200 kilometres north of the Arctic Circle in Saamiland (formerly known as Lapland), the most northerly part of Sweden. Before the arrival of the Ice Hotel there were almost no tourists in this sparsely populated region, where the local people speak Saami, not Swedish, and there is no industry or pollution.

(3) The Ice Hotel is not a permanent building but is rebuilt each winter. Construction of the 5000 square metre building starts in late October when special snow cannons shoot tons of snow onto steel sections. After two days the steel sections are removed leaving solid snow arches five or six metres wide. Over the following weeks the sections are reused to make more arches. Huge ice blocks are carved from the frozen river to make walls and pillars. About 30000 tons of snow and 4000 tons of ice are used to build the hotel.

(4) The story of the Ice Hotel began in the winter of 1989–90. There was an exhibition of ice art in the local village and a cylinder-shaped igloo made of ice was built for an exhibition by French artist Jannot Derid. Some of the visitors decided to sleep on reindeer skins in the igloo and found it a surprisingly relaxing and stimulating environment. Yngve Bergqvist, the owner of the small local inn, realised that others might want to share this unique experience and the concept of the Ice Hotel was born.

(5) Visitors to the Ice Hotel are sometimes nervous about staying in a place where the outside temperature in winter is often minus forty degrees Centigrade. But of course local people have been living in this environment for thousands of years, and conditions inside the Ice Hotel are reasonably comfortable. The temperature is usually around minus four degrees, and guests are provided with specially made sleeping bags and their beds are lined with reindeer skins. To keep visitors amused in the evenings the hotel includes an 'ice cinema' and a well stocked 'ice bar'. During the day the hotel company organises sports activities such as white water rafting, dogsledding and fishing, and there are tours of local villages and 'safaris' to observe reindeer in their natural habitat.

Vocabulary | weather

2 Use the clues to complete the crossword.

Across

1 very hot
5 light rain
6 no clouds
9 rain from time to time
11 not warm or very cold

Down

2 grey sky
3 never the same
4 a light wind
7 adjective from clue 4
8 quite cold
10 move liquid

Grammar | questions

3 Match the questions and answers. Then complete the questions with one word.

1 Have you _____ a holiday this year?
2 Where _____ you go?
3 When _____ you go?
4 _____ did you get there?
5 _____ you go on your own?
6 _____ went with you?
7 How _____ did you go for?
8 What _____ it like?
9 _____ it expensive?
10 _____ you going to go again?

a We flew via Dubai.
b Fantastic!
c Three weeks.
d Yes, probably.
e To Thailand.
f Yes, it was.
g No, I didn't.
h Yes, I have.
i My boyfriend.
j Last January.

4 Put the words in the correct order to make questions.

get when a refund me can you tell I'll
Can you tell me when I'll get a refund?

1 to was who talking she
_____?

2 if my do know you this seat is
_____?

3 much costs it can tell you me how
_____?

4 they car where the did take
_____?

5 ask to the open could I you window
_____?

6 the how you computer do turn off
_____?

7 correct are the answers these
_____?

8 been how you here long have working
_____?

5 Rewrite the direct questions as indirect questions. Start with the words given.

Where are you from?
Can you *tell me where you are from?*

1 What's your email address?
Can you _____
_____?

2 Does Graham Randall live here?
Could I _____
_____?

3 Is this the correct platform for the train to Brighton?
Do you _____
_____?

4 Which seats in the plane have the most legroom?
I'd like to _____
_____.

5 Is the doctor available now?
Can I _____
_____?

6 Where exactly does she live?
Can you explain _____
_____?

7 How much do the tickets cost?
Do you _____
_____?

8 Who is in charge?
Would you tell _____
_____?

Listening

1 a **6.1** Cover the tapescript. Listen to five people talking to a researcher. Match them to the statements A–E.

A used to live abroad ☐

B has seen TV programmes about emigrants ☐

C definitely isn't interested in living abroad ☐

D is planning to live abroad at some point ☐

E would like to live abroad but hasn't got any definite plans ☐

b Listen again and match these descriptions to the people.

1 is a university student ☐

2 had problems with travel documents ☐

3 is in a hurry ☐

4 is worried about being identified ☐

5 has family responsibilities ☐

c Now read the tapescript. Find words and phrases that mean:

1 thought about (*n*) _____

2 make someone leave their home (*v*) _____

3 interested in/fascinated by (*-ed adj + prep*) _____

4 depressing (*adj*) _____

5 giving you a feeling you want to do something (*-ing adj*) _____

6 this is my true feeling/opinion (*phrase*) _____

7 clearly (*adv*) _____

8 chances (*n*) _____

TAPESCRIPT

1

R: Excuse me. Can I ask you some questions about living abroad?

W: Sure.

R: Have you ever considered moving to a foreign country?

W: Not really. I'm quite happy with my life as it is! And I've got four kids, so it would be a bit difficult to uproot them from their schools and things, wouldn't it?

2

R: Hello. I'm doing some research on emigration. Can I talk to you for a minute?

M: OK. If it's quick. I'm a bit late for an appointment.

R: Thanks. Er. Have you ever thought about moving abroad?

M: Yes. I'm quite intrigued by the idea of living somewhere else.

R: Any particular reason?

M: The weather, I suppose. It's so grim here in the winter, isn't it?

R: So you'd prefer somewhere hotter?

M: Probably. But I'm not really sure where ...

3

R: Excuse me. Can I ask you some questions about living in a foreign country?

M: Alright. You don't need my name or anything, do you?

R: No, nothing like that. I'd just like to ask you how you feel about the idea of moving abroad.

M: Oh, yes. I've seen those TV programmes about people moving to Australia. It always looks tempting.

R: Have you ever considered doing it yourself?

M: Myself? I've not really thought about it to be honest.

4

R: Excuse me. Hello. Could I just take a few minutes of your time? I'm doing some research on people emigrating for my college course.

W: Really? I lived in Canada for a year when I was younger.

R: Oh. But obviously you came back ...

W: Well, I had this Canadian boyfriend. But it didn't really work out. And it was really difficult getting the right visas and things ...

5

R: Hi. Would you mind answering a few questions? It'll only take a minute or two.

M: Of course. No problem.

R: Have you ever considered emigrating?

M: I certainly have. I'd love to do it.

R: Why?

M: Well, the job opportunities, really. I'm in the middle of an engineering degree and when I finish I'm going to apply for jobs in the Middle East. There are loads of well-paid engineering posts over there ...

Vocabulary | verb phrases about moving/travelling

2 Match the sentence halves.

1 I've always dreamed about ☐
2 See you later. I'm ☐
3 Make sure you've got your passport and tickets before ☐
4 We hate the cold weather here so we're going ☐
5 Now that I'm eighteen I think it's time ☐
6 She went to Greece and ☐
7 His girlfriend didn't even bother to go to the station ☐
8 We don't have enough bedrooms so we need ☐

a to emigrate.
b to move house.
c off to work.
d to see him off.
e roamed around the beaches.
f setting off.
g living abroad.
h to leave home.

Grammar | comparative & superlative adjectives and adverbs

3 Complete the newspaper article using appropriate comparative or superlative forms of the words in brackets. Add any words that are necessary.

The Ultimate Thrill

With the latest technological developments, new rollercoaster rides

are much (1) _____ (exciting) ever before. But thrill seekers looking for the ultimate rollercoaster ride are now torn between two monster rides on opposite sides of the world. (2) _____ (big) is Steel Dragon 2000 in Nagashima Spaland, a theme park in Japan, about 200 miles west of Tokyo. The ride is over one and a half miles long, lasts four minutes and includes a 68 degree drop. At times riders reach speeds (3) _____ (great) 95 miles per hour. Costing $55 million, the ride is also (4) _____ (expensive) ever built.

Steel Dragon 2000's arch rival is the brand new Kingda Ka ride at Six Flags Great Adventure Park, near Philadelphia, USA. It (5) _____ (not long) as its Japanese competitor, but what it lacks in size it makes up for in speed and height. With riders travelling at up to 128 miles per hour (206 kilometres per hour) it is by far (6) _____ (fast) rollercoaster ride on earth. It is also (7) _____ (tall), with a maximum height of 456 feet (139 metres). But at less than one minute, the ride is much (8) _____ (short) the four-minute experience of Steel Dragon 2000.

4 There is one mistake in each sentence. Find the mistakes and correct them.

1 I think Jeremy's got the most heavy bag.
2 This exercise is bit more difficult than the last one.
3 He was bad hurt in the accident.
4 I'm sorry I arrived so lately; I missed the bus.
5 The Mayback is most expensive car BMW has ever made.
6 They say Seville is always hoter than Madrid.
7 This novel isn't as interesting than his previous one.
8 Mobile phones are quite lot cheaper than they used to be.
9 Antonio lives more far from the school than I do.
10 I'm not as taller as my sister.
11 She speaks Italian very good.
12 That was the most bad DVD I've ever watched.

Pronunciation

5 a `6.2` Are the underlined sounds in each sentence the same (S) or different (D)? Listen and check.

1 Life at university is hard<u>er</u> th<u>an</u> at home, but it isn't <u>as</u> hard <u>as</u> at school. ☐
2 He's isn't <u>as</u> f<u>a</u>t as his f<u>a</u>ther. ☐

b `6.3` Mark the underlined sounds in the sentences the same (S) or different (D). Then listen and check.

1 This h<u>a</u>t isn't <u>as</u> expensive as that plate. ☐
2 I worked hard<u>er</u> th<u>an</u> my brother. ☐
3 They're not <u>as</u> c<u>er</u>tain <u>as</u> they need to be. ☐
4 The fridge w<u>as</u> more expensive th<u>an</u> the cook<u>er</u>. ☐
5 Is it <u>as</u> expensive <u>as</u> the morning cl<u>a</u>ss? ☐

Vocabulary

1 There is one mistake in each sentence. Find the mistakes and correct them.

1 I didn't go with a group; I went as an independence traveller.

2 Experiencing culture shocked can be one of the most difficult parts of living in a foreign country.

3 Do you make itchy feet or are you happy to stay in your home town?

4 My sister has always loved travelling – she was bitten by the journey bug as a teenager.

5 I love the unknown; I adore going through uncharted territory.

6 We never go on organised tours, we prefer to wonder around on our own.

Present Perfect Simple and Continuous

2 Complete the text about Bono using Past Simple, Present Perfect or Present Perfect Continuous forms of the verbs in brackets.

BONO (1) _____ (be) a rock star for the last 25 years. But recently he (2) _____ (become) famous for something completely different – his work for charity. Since 2004 Bono (3) _____ (lead) the fight against poverty in Africa, trying to get more people to understand that continent's terrible problems of famine and disease. For several years now he (4) _____ (appear) regularly on TV shows and at international events, attempting to get the world's media to pay attention to this issue. He (5) _____ (have) meetings with many world leaders and in 2005 he (6) _____ (help) organise the Live8 concerts in London and around the world. Bono lives in Dublin but spends much of his time travelling with his group, U2. Bono believes his position as an international celebrity (7) _____ (give) him a unique opportunity to influence young people. He (8) _____ (visit) Africa several times and these experiences (9) _____ (clearly influence) his political views. In 2003 Bono (10) _____ (meet) Nelson Mandela in Cape Town and in July 2005 he (11) _____ (speak) to world leaders at the G8 Conference in Scotland, helping to influence their decisions on reducing Africa's debt. Critics sometimes say that Bono (12) _____ (only do) this for the last few years to compensate for his group's declining popularity. But with their latest CD high in the charts, this can hardly be the case.

Vocabulary

3 Use the clues to complete the crossword.

Across

3 It's a ___ story, full of twists and turns that keep you hooked.

4 I can't stand cabbage soup, I think it's ___.

7 Babies are often ___ by brightly coloured objects.

8 That new horror film was absolutely ___.

9 It's very ___ when people push in front of you at the supermarket check-out.

10 A lot of people would feel ___ by running a marathon but I take it in my stride.

Down

1 I'm a bit ___ about Miriam. Is there something wrong with her?

2 She found the task ___ but she managed to achieve it in the end.

5 You shouldn't have told the children that scary story, they were ___.

6 Picasso was ___ by African tribal art.

4 Match the words 1–8 with their opposites a–h.

1	humid	a	grey
2	clear	b	settled
3	bright	c	warm
4	drizzle	d	calm
5	cool	e	dry
6	chilly	f	pour
7	breezy	g	scorching
8	changeable	h	overcast

Questions

5 There are eight incorrect questions in this dialogue. Find the mistakes and correct them.

Woman:	I'm doing some market research. Could I ask you some questions?
Man:	Sure.
Woman:	Where went you for your holidays?
5 **Man:**	We went to Florida.
Woman:	Who did go on holiday with you?
Man:	My girlfriend.
Woman:	Can I ask what is her name?
Man:	Of course. Her name's Lucy.
10 **Woman:**	Could you tell me what does she for a living?
Man:	Yes. She's a hotel receptionist.
Woman:	Do you know how old she is?
Man:	She's twenty-one.
15 **Woman:**	Can you tell me is she British?
Man:	No. She's Australian.
Woman:	How long she has lived here?
Man:	About six months.
Woman:	I'd like to know where did you meet her.
20 **Man:**	We met at a party.
Woman:	Why did you go to Florida?
Man:	Well, we wanted to see Miami and Key West.
25 **Woman:**	Would you tell me how long did you stay in Florida?
Man:	We stayed there for three weeks.

Vocabulary

6 Choose the correct alternative.

1 The neighbours were very noisy so I had to *move/change* house.

2 When I left for university my parents came to the station to see me *out/off*.

3 Their daughter lives *abroad/outside* so they don't see her very often.

4 Over a million Scots *migrated/emigrated* to the USA in the 19th century.

5 The police found a small child roaming *round/around* in the streets.

6 You must be very excited about your trip. When do you *go/set* off?

7 When I was sixteen I left *home/house* to join the army.

8 I can't talk now; I'm *off/out* to meet my brother from the bus station.

9 Are you going *over/away* for the bank holiday or are you staying here?

10 She *walked/set* out after they had a terrible argument.

Comparative & superlative adjectives and adverbs

7 Tick (✓) the phrases which can be used to fill the gaps and put a cross (✗) by those that cannot. Sometimes more than one is possible.

1 I don't think Barcelona is ___ Malaga.
   A as sunny as ☐   B sunnyer than ☐
   C sunnier than ☐

2 My new mobile is ___ my old one.
   A more good than ☐   B a lot better than ☐
   C many better than ☐

3 Bill Gates is ___ in America.
   A the richest man ☐
   B the man richest ☐
   C the most rich man ☐

4 This model is ___ in the shop.
   A the less expensive ☐
   B the most less expensive ☐
   C the least expensive ☐

5 Los Angeles is usually ___ San Francisco.
   A not as hot as ☐   B hoter than ☐
   C hotter than ☐

6 Ella arrived ___ the others.
   A a bit later than ☐   B much later than ☐
   C just as late as ☐

7 Did you drive ___ we did?
   A more far than ☐   B as far as ☐
   C further than ☐

8 He takes life ___ most people his age.
   A more serious than ☐
   B more seriously than ☐
   C just as serious as ☐

Vocabulary

8 Complete the sentences with expressions with *go*.

1 Which car did you decide to go _____ in the end?

2 I'd love to _____ a go at ice-skating; I've never tried it before.

3 Do you think Johan will be able to _____ a go of the new business?

4 Of course we'll pay – that goes _____ saying.

5 Trust me; I never go _____ on a promise.

6 I hope you like this CD. I went to great _____ to find it for you.

7 What's going _____ in the Big Brother house?

8 Kieran's always on _____ go – she never seems to stand still!

7.1 Excess

Listening

1 a **7.1** Cover the tapescript. Listen to the conversation and answer the questions.

1 How many speakers are there?

2 What are they trying to decide?

3 What do they decide to do in the end?

b Listen again and tick (✓) the correct column.

		Tom	Ben	Alice
1	fancies eating a burger	☐	☐	☐
2	likes fried chicken	☐	☐	☐
3	suggests going to a pizza place	☐	☐	☐
4	loves pizza	☐	☐	☐
5	is supposed to be on a diet	☐	☐	☐
6	thinks burgers aren't as fattening as pizzas	☐	☐	☐
7	doesn't like vegetarian burgers	☐	☐	☐
8	loves king prawns	☐	☐	☐

c Now look at the tapescript. Find the following adjectives and phrases and write them in the correct column.

> greasy   to be sick of something   starving
> delicious   not too keen on   disgusting
> yummy   tasteless   ravenous
> I could eat a horse   scrumptious

Feeling very hungry	Positive opinion	Negative opinion

TAPESCRIPT

Tom: I haven't eaten since lunch time and I'm starving. Do either of you feel like popping out for a take-away?

Ben: Great idea, Tom. I'm ravenous.

Alice: Me too. I could eat a horse! Could you get something for me as well?

Tom: What do you fancy?

Alice: Um. I'm not sure. A burger, I suppose.

Tom: OK. What about you, Ben?

Ben: I'm not too keen on burgers, really. How about fried chicken or something?

Alice: Oh, that's disgusting, so greasy.

Tom: Actually, I was thinking of pizza for myself. There's that new pizza place near the station. It's called Pizza Delight, or something like that. Does that appeal to either of you?

Alice: Yummy. I love pizza.

Ben: Yuk. I'm sick of pizzas. I've had them twice this week already.

Tom: I thought you were on a diet, Ben.

Alice: Yeah. He's on the pizza diet!

Ben: Very funny, Alice. And I suppose burgers are super healthy, are they?

Alice: Well I'm sure they're not as fattening as pizzas. Anyway, I was going to have a vegetarian burger.

Ben: A vegetarian burger? They're completely tasteless. Like eating cardboard!

Tom: Look. There's no point arguing. We need to agree on something.

Ben: What about kebabs?

Tom: Oh no. I had one of those a couple of days ago and it gave me a bit of a stomach-ache.

Alice: I know. What about Chinese?

Ben: Good idea. There's a Chinese take-away in Arnold Street. It's just around the corner from the supermarket. They do that delicious Peking Duck ...

Tom: Yes. And they've got those scrumptious king prawns. Great. Chinese it is!

Grammar | countable and uncountable nouns

2 Choose the correct words to complete the text.

Riverside Technical College
Student Facilities

Here are just (1) ___ the facilities we provide for our students. We hope you'll agree we have something to offer everyone!

Computer and Internet Centre

You're always connected at Riverside! We have (2) ___ computers available, all with free access to the Internet. There are (3) ___ printers too – so you can print out your essays with ease. And if you need (4) ___ advice, we have two full-time computer technicians available.

Student Café and Bar

(5) ___ students enjoy taking their lunch here. We have a range of delicious snacks, including healthy salads and sandwiches. We're open until midnight, so why not invite (6) ___ friends and spend the evening with us? Or just pop in for (7) ___ coffee and a slice of our homemade cake.

College Sports Centre

Why not improve your health with (8) ___ exercise? Riverside has an extensive range of sports facilities. We have state of the art exercise machines in our gym and a fabulous heated swimming pool. In fact, some of our students spend (9) ___ their free time here. There are (10) ___ colleges in the country which can rival our sports provision, and it's all free for students!

1 A few   B some   C a few of
2 A much   B many   C any
3 A lots of   B any   C much
4 A an   B many   C some
5 A Few   B A lot of   C Much
6 A a few   B a little   C few
7 A a   B a piece of   C little
8 A many   B little   C a little
9 A a great deal of   B many   C a lot
10 A a few   B little   C few

3 Decide if the sentences in each pair are correct (✓) or incorrect (✗). Sometimes both sentences are correct.

1 A I eat two eggs every morning. ☐
   B She got egg all down the front of her dress. ☐
2 A He bought me some chocolates for my birthday. ☐
   B She's diabetic so she can't eat chocolate. ☐
3 A I need some legal advice. ☐
   B The doctor gave her three advices. ☐
4 A My new car has excellent equipments. ☐
   B Will you bring the camping equipment? ☐
5 A Pedro's knowledge of computers is impressive. ☐
   B Knowledge are very important in the modern world. ☐
6 A I often feel nostalgic for the old times. ☐
   B There never seems to be enough time. ☐

Vocabulary | food and cooking

4 **a** Combine words from box A with words from box B to make ten expressions.

A	B
an electric grilled	milk eggs cook
grated a wooden	cheese recipe pan
a talented	cooker sausages
a complicated	plate spoon
scrambled a china	
sour a frying	

b Complete the sentences using expressions from Ex. 4a.

1 I love putting _____ on top of pasta.
2 We don't have gas in our area so we had to buy _____ for the kitchen.
3 We're having a barbeque with _____ and burgers.
4 Would you prefer toast or _____ for breakfast tomorrow?
5 Edwina's husband is _____.
6 The smell of _____ is revolting.

Reading

1 **a** Read the text quickly and choose the best title.

1 Impressionist Paintings at Sotheby's
2 The Story of Sotheby's
3 Britain's Greatest Auction House

b Read the text again and match the information 1–8 with the information a–h.

1 Sotheby's ☐
2 Samuel Baker ☐
3 James Christie ☐
4 the auction of Talleyrand's library ☐
5 Peter Wilson ☐
6 the first public auction of impressionist masterpieces ☐
7 Parke-Bernet ☐
8 Alfred Taubman ☐

a John Sotheby's rival
b 1958
c chairman of Sotheby's
d the most famous auction house
e an American businessman
f John Sotheby's uncle
g 1793
h a New York auction house

c Find words or phrases in the text that mean:

1 worth a lot of money (*adj*) _____
2 state an opinion that others might disagree with (*v*) _____
3 competitor (*n*) _____
4 copy someone's example (*phrase*) _____
5 effect/impression/influence (*n*) _____
6 best/highest quality examples of works of art (*n*) _____
7 time when the economy is bad (*n*) _____
8 completely (*adj*) _____

(1) There is little doubt that Sotheby's is the oldest and most famous auction house in the world. It has been going for more than two and a half centuries and has sold many of the most famous and valuable treasures and works of art ever created. Its rivals might disagree but many would argue that the international art market as it exists today (1) _____ (create) by Sotheby's. The idea of enormously valuable works of art being sold at public auction is something we take for granted, but in fact it is a relatively new phenomenon. So how did it all come about?

(2) It all began back in 1744 when a book dealer called Samuel Baker opened a small book store in the Strand in London. After his death in 1778 the business (2) _____ (take over) by his nephew, John Sotheby. Sotheby had a great rival, James Christie, who (3) _____ (start) the Christie's auction house in 1776. Buying and selling things at auction was made fashionable by James Christie but John Sotheby was quick to follow his lead. In 1793 he

auctioned Talleyrand's library and in 1823 he (4) _____ (score) a public relations triumph by auctioning Napoleon's collection of books from St Helena.

(3) Sotheby's business grew throughout the 19th century but it was only in the middle of the 20th century that Sotheby's began to make a huge impact internationally. In 1958 its charismatic chairman, Peter Wilson, (5) _____ (organise) the first ever public auction of impressionist masterpieces by Cezanne, Renoir and Van Gogh. Before that time extremely valuable works such as

these (6) _____ (sell) privately or through dealers. Wilson turned the whole auction into a fashionable event. He sent invitations to film stars and politicians and held the auction in the evening. Journalists from the leading papers (7) _____ (invite) and everyone was asked to wear black tie or evening dress. Not surprisingly, the auction got a huge amount of publicity and the prices set new records.

(4) With its growing reputation in London Sotheby's decided to expand into the American market and bought the New York auction house Parke-Bernet. But things began to go wrong during the oil crisis and the recession of the 1970s and the company started to get into financial difficulties. In 1971 they even tried to raise money by launching a Sotheby's brand of cigarette. Eventually, in 1983 Sotheby's (8) _____ (buy) by American businessman, Alfred Taubman. Based in Detroit, Taubman transformed Sotheby's into a wholly American company. It was certainly a long way from the little bookshop in the Strand.

Vocabulary | verb phrases about money

2 One word in each sentence is incorrect. Find the word and correct it.

1 It's a good idea to keep the refund when you buy expensive things.

2 If we buy ten of these, can we get a bargain of 10%?

3 Auctions are fun but I do get nervous when people start haggling for something I want.

4 I want to buy a new computer but I can't worth it yet.

5 I love buying things in street markets – it's great fun bidding with the market traders.

6 They're moving house next year so they're not sure if it's afford buying a new sofa.

Grammar | passives

3 Complete the text in Ex. 1 using appropriate active or passive forms of the verbs in brackets.

4 Rewrite the sentences in *italics* in the text using <u>only</u> passive forms.

Money Factsheet 8

(1) *How does the Mint make coins?*

Long sheets of metal arrive at the mint.
(2) *Somebody feeds the metal strips into a cutting machine.*
(3) *The cutting machine cuts the metal into round shapes called 'blanks'.*
(4) *After the machine has cut them out somebody heats the blanks in a furnace.*
(5) *Somebody washes the blanks while somebody is heating them.*
The hot blanks go into a pressing machine and (6) *the machine stamps each coin with a pattern on both sides.*
(7) *Somebody cools the coins and a special machine counts them.*
(8) *Somebody distributes the coins to the banks.*

1 *How are coins made?*
2 _____
3 _____
4 _____
5 _____
6 _____
7 _____
8 _____

5 Rewrite each sentence beginning with the words given.

Peter published the report last year.

The report *was published last year.*

1 The doctor has given Alison a new prescription.
Alison _____.

2 You mustn't open the present until your birthday.
The present _____.

3 The police are investigating the crime.
The crime _____.

4 They are going to open the hotel in November.
The hotel _____.

5 We will drive the children to the party.
The children _____.

6 You can see my house from the top of the hill.
My house _____.

7 Somebody was watching them.
They _____.

8 They haven't released that DVD yet.
That DVD _____.

9 Somebody might have seen the burglar.
The burglar _____.

10 They didn't take anything.
Nothing _____.

Writing/How to ... | write a letter of complaint

6 Rewrite this informal letter as a formal letter of complaint. Look at page 163 of the Students' Book to help you.

Dear James O'Brien

I'm writing to tell you about a mobile phone I bought in your shop the other day.

When I got home it didn't work. I was really shocked because it cost €250!

Please send me another phone or give me a refund immediately.

I'd love to get a reply soon.

Love from

Mandy Smith

Listening

1 **a** **7.2** Cover the tapescript. Listen to five people talking about animals. Match each person with an animal from the box. Three animals are not needed.

> snake cats spider tropical fish
> mouse horse goldfish dog

1 _____   3 _____   5 _____
2 _____   4 _____

b Listen again and match the statements with the animals 1–5 in Ex. 1a.

1 is always hungry _____
2 lives in a big field _____
3 need a lot of care and attention _____
4 loves going for walks _____
5 doesn't jump any more _____
6 provide companionship _____
7 moves very slowly _____
8 costs a lot of money to maintain _____

c Now look at the tapescript. Find the words in the box and put them in the correct columns. There are three words in each column.

> dart crawl tank sinuous gentle
> kennel trot playful stable

Ways animals move (verbs)	Places animals live (nouns)	Animal characteristics (adjectives)

TAPESCRIPT

1

Well, I'm not sure you'd call them pets, really. I mean you don't have to take them to the vet, or for walks, obviously. But they do require quite a lot of care and attention. I seem to spend ages cleaning out the pond and repairing the water filters. It's a nightmare in autumn with all the fallen leaves. And in winter you have to make sure the surface doesn't get covered in ice. But they do give me a lot of pleasure, watching them darting around.

2

We've had him for about four years now. He's got a kennel in the back garden. His name's Wolfie. David bought him for the children, really. Everyone knows retrievers are great with kids – so gentle and playful. He's got beautiful blond fur and he loves being cuddled. Of course, he adores being taken for walks – which is a great excuse for us to get some exercise as well! The only downside is the amount of food he eats. And whatever we give him, he always seems to be starving.

3

Some people think keeping a reptile is a bit weird, but you'd be surprised at how popular it is. I know loads of people that do it. I got Sarah from a friend and I wasn't too sure about it at first. It's a bit of a fuss because you have to have a big tank and keep it at a certain temperature. And when she sheds her skin it's a bit disgusting. But I think she's beautiful – the way she moves is so slow and sinuous. I love letting her crawl up my arms and around my neck.

4

When I was younger I used to take her out jumping and things, but I hurt my back a few years ago so now we just go for walks. Or a bit of a gentle trot if I'm feeling energetic! We've got a big field behind the house so she's got plenty of room, and there's a small stable for the winter months. Big animals are always quite expensive to look after, but I think it's worth it. I mean I get plenty of exercise, and I feel we have a really strong bond. I certainly wouldn't let anyone else ride her.

5

I never had any children, but I think in some ways they're better than children. A lot less trouble! I've got two at the moment, Tiddles and Spark. Tiddles is just a kitten, really. Now that I'm retired I don't really get out much so they're ideal for me, and they're much easier to look after than dogs. They're pretty independent but they give me a lot of companionship. I talk to them all the time, which is a bit stupid I know, but at least I don't get lonely.

Grammar | *have/get something done*

2 Complete the picture labels using forms of *have/get something done*. Use verbs from box A and words/phrases from box B.

A	B
check paint do test service wash	car blood pressure house boiler hair eyes

1 Mrs Alderson _____ every month.
2 Daniel _____ once a week.
3 The Smiths _____ every five years.
4 Liz _____ once every six months.
5 Mr Grant _____ when he goes to the clinic.
6 We _____ before the beginning of winter.

3 Rewrite the sentences using the words in brackets.

He needs to finish that project soon. (done)
He needs to get that project done soon.

1 Somebody left the bag behind. (got)
_____

2 The maid washes Linda's clothes. (has)
_____

3 They forward my post to me. (I)
_____

4 Will somebody cut your hair this week? (get)
_____

5 How often do they clean your windows? (you)
_____

6 I should finish my homework by six o'clock. (done)
_____

Vocabulary | animals

4 Use the clues to complete the crossword with animal words.

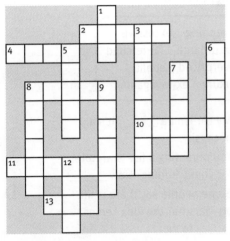

Across

2 they can be very sharp
4 it lives in the sea
8 to take the bull by the ___
10 symbol of the USA
11 they keep birds warm
13 if you see this above the water it could be a shark

Down

1 planes and birds do this
3 cats have very long ones
5 straight from the ___'s mouth
6 the biggest animal
7 birds couldn't fly without them
8 toenails for a horse
9 lots of people are afraid of this insect
12 it's at the back of a horse or dog

Pronunciation

5 **7.3** Look at the <u>underlined</u> sounds in each group of words. Circle the odd one out. Then listen and check.

1 h<u>or</u>ns   cl<u>aws</u>   c<u>ow</u>
2 f<u>ea</u>thers   b<u>ea</u>k   b<u>ear</u>
3 w<u>i</u>ngs   f<u>i</u>ns   t<u>i</u>ger
4 <u>ea</u>gle   wh<u>a</u>le   t<u>ai</u>l
5 h<u>or</u>se   f<u>ur</u>   p<u>aw</u>

Vocabulary

1 Complete the sentences using words from the box. Two words are not needed.

> spending excessive
> extra-large far-fetched
> overpriced spoilt
> luxury extravagant

1 My car isn't a _____; it's a necessity.

2 You're renting a five-star hotel for your wedding? How _____!

3 Some people say there is life on Mars but the idea seems _____ to me.

4 After we moved we went on a _____ spree and bought lots of new furniture.

5 Don't buy anything from that shop – all their goods are very _____.

6 I think it's greedy to order _____ portions in restaurants.

Countable and uncountable nouns

2 Eight of the sentences contain mistakes. Find the mistakes and correct them.

1 Our shop stocks luggages from all over the world.

2 There are few places as beautiful as Kashmir.

3 There isn't many traffic around here on Sundays.

4 May I have little sugar in my coffee, please?

5 I'd like to have a lots of money.

6 They're not very busy, they only have a few work this week.

7 They don't have much money but they're happy.

8 Would you like a spaghetti, or do you prefer rice?

9 You can invite few of your friends to the party if you like.

10 The college offers much courses on foreign languages.

Vocabulary

3 Use the clues to complete the crossword.

Across

4 Heat the milk in a small ___.

5 You have to ___ the mixture quickly until it becomes stiff.

7 I don't eat meat. I'm a ___.

8 Don't cook my steak for very long, I like it __.

12 The soup isn't __ enough, add a little more.

13 This vegetable contains a lot of vitamins.

14 It's a fruit which we often serve with cream.

15 I don't put sugar in tea or coffee – I hate ___ drinks.

Down

1 They say ___ are very good for you.

2 You haven't cooked this, it's completely ___.

3 Coffee without sugar has this taste.

6 Do you prefer to ___ eggs or fry them?

9 This tastes delicious. Could you give me the ___?

10 I like to ___ a little parmesan cheese on top of my pasta.

11 Would you like a ___ of cake?

4 Complete the sentences using words from the box.

> afford bargain bidding discount
> haggling worth receipt refund

1 I only paid €10 for this DVD – I got a _____!

2 I'd love to get a new car but I'm not sure I can _____ it.

3 We love visiting the local markets and _____ for things.

4 I'm afraid you cannot return the goods if you do not have a _____.

5 Don't interrupt him; he's _____ for something on an Internet auction site.

6 We are offering a 20% _____ to any customers who buy more than five CDs.

7 It's a really expensive trip but we think it's _____ it.

8 Due to the cancellation of tonight's performance we are offering a full _____ to all ticket holders.

Passives

5 You have just booked a holiday on the Internet. Read the web page and complete the sentences below. Use appropriate passive forms.

Thank you
**for making a
booking with**

Your booking reference is HJ980L

We have debited €450 from your credit card. For your security we use 128 KB protection software for all credit card payments.

We are sending your itinerary by email. We will send your flight tickets by first class post. Please note the following:

- You must bring your passport to check-in one hour before departure.
- You cannot change the date and time of your flights.
- You can pre-book seats on the website.
- GoAway Travel does not allow smoking on any of its flights.
- You may purchase meals on the plane.
- The price includes transfers from the airport.

Please see our FAQs if you have any further queries.

---

1 €450 _____
   _____.

2 128 KB protection software _____
   _____.

3 Your itinerary _____
   _____.

4 Your tickets _____
   _____.

5 Your passport _____
   _____.

6 The date and time of your flights _____
   _____.

7 Seats _____
   _____.

8 Smoking_____
   _____.

9 Meals _____
   _____.

10 Transfers from the airport _____
   _____.

have/get something done

6 Complete each sentence with one word.

1 I _____ the central heating checked last month so it should be fine now.
2 She never received her new credit card – it must have _____ lost in the post.
3 I'm sorry about spilling wine on your jacket. I'll have it _____ for you.
4 Tell the boss that Jamie will _____ the report finished by four o'clock.
5 Have you got the broken chair _____?
6 He _____ arrested by the local police.
7 Do you _____ your photocopying done locally?
8 I like to have my hair _____ by Silvia. She's the best stylist in the salon.
9 I'm going to get my photo _____; I need it for the job application.
10 It blocks the light so we are _____ that big tree removed.

Vocabulary

7 **a** Circle the incorrect word in each group.

1 A bull has: horns hooves fin tail
2 A cat has: whiskers beak paws claws
3 An eagle has: wings paws feathers beak
4 A bear has: fur paws hooves claws

b Complete the sentences.

1 She was in such a bad mood she was like a _____ with a _____ head.
2 Don't ask grandma to read the instructions; she's as _____ as a _____.

8 Choose the correct alternative.

1 It doesn't take long to prepare, just *rewarm/reheat* it in the microwave.
2 He's got a fantastic job with a huge *multinational/manynational* company.
3 Can I have the *ex-large/extra-large* burger, please?
4 We thought the seats on the plane were very *uncomfortable/incomfortable*.
5 Sue's *bilanguaged/bilingual*; she speaks English and German equally well.
6 The children get very badly behaved when they're *extra-tired/overtired*.
7 Have you seen your *ex-boyfriend/exboyfriend* recently?
8 The film was *monotonous/monologue* and quite boring.
9 That chicken was *less-cooked/undercooked* – it was pink in the middle.
10 I've just bought a *multipurpose/monopurpose* printer. It can print, scan and photocopy.

Reading

1 **a** Read the text quickly and choose the best heading for each paragraph. Two headings are not needed.

A   The Fight for Freedom

B   Independence

C   Studying in London

D   Introduction

E   Gandhi's Legacy

F   Gandhi's Early Life

G   Life in Prison

H   Philososphy

b Read the text again and decide if these statements are true (T) or false (F).

1   Gandhi was president of India. F

2   Gandhi worked in South Africa. T

3   South Africa used to be part of the British empire. T

4   Local people were sometimes treaded badly in the colonies. F

5   The British were never able to put Gandhi in prison. F

6   Some elements of Satyagraha come from Hinduism. T

7   Gandhi wanted India to be mainly Hindu. F

8   A religious extremist killed Gandhi. T

c Write brief notes to complete this time-line of Gandhi's life.

1869	*born in Porbandar,*
1893	worked i South Africa
1915	returned to india
1947	India achived independence
1948	Gandhi's death

Leading by Example

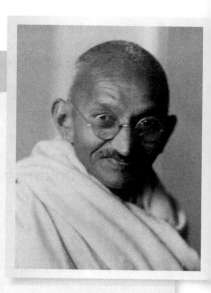

① ~~E~~

Gandhi is one of history's great leaders. But unlike other leaders he never led an army, he was never a president or prime minister and he never used force or violence to impose his leadership on people. His principle of leadership was simple – he led by example. He believed that the best way to influence events was through peaceful protest rather than by violent revolution or bloodshed.

② ~~D~~

Mohandas Karamchand Gandhi was born on 2nd October 1869 in Porbandar in western India. He was sent to England to study law and was offered a job in South Africa after he qualified in 1893. At that time both India and South Africa were colonies of Britain. Working as a lawyer, Gandhi soon began to experience the prejudice that local people suffered under the colonial regime.

③ ~~A~~ G

Gandhi returned to India in 1915, determined to fight against colonialism and injustice. He realised that Indians would never be able to build a fair society until they had independence from the British empire. He joined the Indian nationalist movement and began to fight for Indian independence. The British regarded Gandhi as a troublemaker and he was arrested many times. Rather than resist, Gandhi was quite prepared to be sent to prison for his beliefs. Altogether he spent more than seven years behind bars.

④ H

Most independence movements in history have depended on violence and revolution to achieve their aims. Gandhi was sure that the same effect could be achieved through non-violent protest and a policy of civil disobedience. He developed a philosophy known as 'Satyagraha' which was partly based on the teachings of Hinduism. According to Satyagraha the best way to change society was through peaceful means. Through his own behaviour Gandhi provided an example of this philosophy in action.

⑤ B

After more than thirty years of struggle India eventually achieved independence in 1947. Gandhi's policy of peaceful protests, strikes, trade boycotts and civil disobedience had worked. Gandhi wanted India to be a single country which included all races and religions but his wish was not granted. The Indian sub-continent was split into two states – the mainly Hindu India and the largely Muslim Pakistan.

⑥ _____

Gandhi's belief in religious freedom was to cost him his life. On 30th January 1948 he was assassinated by a young Hindu fanatic, Nathuram Godse. But his legacy was to last long after his death. Gandhi's philosophy of peaceful protest and civil disobedience has been an inspiration to numerous people around the world. By his own actions he showed that the best leaders are those who lead by example rather than by force.

Grammar | *It's time/I'd rather/I'd better*

2 Tick (✓) the sentence which has the same meaning as the sentence in *italics*.

1 *It's time you went to bed.*
   A You should be in bed by now. ✓
   B You are already in bed. ☐

2 *I'd rather take the bus.*
   A There is no other way to get there. ☐
   B I prefer buses to trains. ✓

3 *We'd better take the earlier flight.*
   A We prefer early flights. ☐
   B The later flight might not arrive in time. ✓

4 *Would you rather I replied by email?*
   A I prefer to send emails. ☐
   B Do you want me to send an email? ✓

5 *It's high time you looked for a job.*
   A You've been looking but you haven't found the perfect job yet. ☐
   B You are unemployed. ✓

6 *I'd rather she didn't come.*
   A I don't want her to come. ✓
   B She doesn't want to come. ☐

7 *You'd better take the car.*
   A There's a bus strike today. ✓
   B You prefer driving. ☐

8 *It's about time we left.*
   A It's quite late. ✓
   B We left on time. ☐

3 Rewrite the sentences using the words in brackets.

1 I really think you should move to a bigger flat. (high)

   _____

2 You should take an umbrella. (better)

   _____

3 I prefer going the cinema. (rather)

   _____

4 John needs to get a better computer. (about)

   _____

5 Do you want me to bring my camera? (would)

   _____

6 I would prefer her not to smoke. (didn't)

   _____

7 I don't like working at the weekend. (rather)

   _____

8 I think it's safer if you have the salad. (you'd)

   _____

Vocabulary | describing personality

4 Use the clues to complete the crossword with words to describe personality.

Across

1 Carol's really high ___; she needs expensive presents all the time!

5 I've got strong ideas about everything; I suppose I'm pretty ___.

6 He doesn't have any secrets. He's very ___ and honest.

10 Actors love an audience because they like to be the centre of ___.

11 Dorinda's ___; she likes meeting new people and she talks to everybody.

12 We always laugh when Jake tells a story because he's so ___.

13 My boss is very single-___; he never gets distracted.

Down

1 My girlfriend tricks people into doing what she wants; she's very ___.

2 Lizzie never makes a fuss or complains; she's very ___-going.

3 ___ people always do what they want and refuse to listen to advice.

4 To succeed in business you need to be ___-to-earth and realistic.

7 I wish I could be more ___ but I tend to let other people take the lead.

8 Juanita goes out to clubs every night, she's a real ___ animal.

9 You shouldn't be a ___; try to be more assertive and independent.

H W

Listening

1 a 〔8.1〕 Cover the tapescript. Listen to Amanda and Steven and answer the questions.

1 Where are they? *they are in the gym*
2 What is Amanda's job? *she is a trainer*
3 What are Steven's aims? *to loes weit*

b Listen again and complete each statement with one word.

1 Steven has been training for _six_ weeks. *five*
2 He hasn't done any real exercise for _more than_ years.
3 Steven thinks three months is an _awfully_ long time.
4 He is _still_ eating desserts.
5 He _so_ hungry all the time.
6 Amanda asks Steven about his _energy_ levels.
7 Steven used to feel _lethargic_ in the afternoons.
8 Amanda hasn't prepared the _nutrition_ sheet for Steven yet.

c Now read the tapescript. Match the phrases in *italics* with the reporting verbs in the box.

> ask   admit   complain   promise   remind   explain   suggest

TAPESCRIPT

Amanda:	Come on Steven, keep going.
Steven:	This is exhausting …
Amanda:	One more repetition. You can do it … Great. Well done. Let's take a short break now.
Steven:	Phew! Good idea!
Amanda:	You're doing really well, you know.
Steven:	(1) *I'm still finding it quite difficult.*
Amanda:	Well, you can't expect to get completely fit in just a month.
Steven:	(2) *Actually, it's been six weeks.*
Amanda:	Six weeks then. You know it usually takes about three months to get fit. After all, you haven't done any real exercise <u>for more than five years</u>, so you've got some catching up to do.
Steven:	Mm. It seems an <u>awfully</u> long time.
Amanda:	Be positive. We're almost half way there.
Steven:	(3) *How long before I start to lose weight?*
Amanda:	That depends. Have you cut out all those sweet snacks?
Steven:	Er, sort of. But I'm afraid I'm <u>still</u> eating desserts. I just feel so hungry all the time.
Amanda:	(4) *How about trying fruit instead of a dessert?*
Steven:	OK. (5) *I'll give it a try.*
Amanda:	(6) *If you cut down the amount of sugar you eat, you're bound to lose weight.* Now, how about your <u>energy</u> levels? Are you still feeling <u>lethargic</u> in the afternoons?
Steven:	No, that's definitely improved. I haven't really felt as tired as I used to.
	That's great.
	Oh, have you prepared that nutrition sheet for me?
	…orry. (7) *I'm afraid I forgot.* I'll do it next week. So, are you …ady to move on to the next machine?
	…h. You trainers are such slave drivers!

Vocabulary | adjectives and intensifiers

2 Complete the sentences using intensifiers. Use *absolutely* with non-gradable adjectives and *really* with gradable adjectives.

1 Saturday's game is _absolutely_ vital for our hopes of promotion.
2 I always feel _really_ hungry after swimming.
3 I often feel _really_ tired at the end of the day.
4 Terry was _absolutely_ devastated when the factory closed down.
5 Suzanne was _absolutely_ exhausted after the race.
6 Poor Joe! He's _really_ upset about his exam results.
7 What's there to eat? I'm _absolutely_ starving!
8 Take your time to decide. This is a _really_ important decision for you.

Pronunciation

3 a 〔8.2〕 <u>Underline</u> the two words that have the main stress in these sentences. Then listen and check.

1 When the children got back from the park they were <u>absolutely filthy</u>.
2 Clare was <u>really devastated</u> when she heard the news.

b 〔8.3〕 Look at the completed sentences Ex. 2 above. <u>Underline</u> the two words with the main stress in each sentence. Then listen and check.

Grammar | reported speech

4 **8.4** Cover the tapescript. Listen to six examples of direct speech from the conversation in Ex. 1. Write them in reported speech, using reporting verbs from the box.

> admit ask promise suggest ~~warn~~ explain

1 Amanda _____

2 Amanda *warned Steven (that) he couldn't expect to get completely fit in just a month.*

3 Steven _____

4 Amanda _____

5 Steven _____

6 Amanda _____

5 Choose the correct words to complete the sentences.

1 When we were young our parents _C_ not to talk to strangers.
  A told   B told to us   C told us

2 James asked me what _A_ for my birthday.
  A I wanted   B did I want   C wanted me

3 My girlfriend asked me _B_ go to the party with her.
  A will I   B if I would   C that I would

4 He said _B_ already bought the tickets.
  A me he had   B he had   C to me he had

5 The sales assistant suggested _A_ a new MP3 player.
  A buying   B to buy   C me buying

6 Davina asked me _A_ been the day before.
  A where I had   B where had I   C where was I

7 The police officer warned me _C_ so fast in future.
  A not driving   B not to driving   C not to drive

8 Michael asked us _B_ the film last Wednesday.
  A did we enjoy   B if we had enjoyed   C if we enjoy

9 She asked me whether _B_ a school uniform when I was at infant school.
  A I must wear   B I had to wear   C did I have to wear

10 The criminal promised _A_ out of trouble.
  A to stay   B staying   C he will stay

6 Report these examples of direct speech using suitable reporting verbs from the box. Use each verb once.

> admit decide explain promise ~~remind~~ suggest warn

David Don't forget to lock the back door.

David reminded me to lock the back door.

1 **My brother** Why don't we go out for a meal?
My brother suggested going out for a meal

2 **John** I can't come because I have to work that evening.
Jon explained that he couldn't come because he had to work that

3 **The children** We'll never do it again.
The children promised that they would never do it again

4 **The lifeguard** Swimming there can be very dangerous.
The lifeguart warned that swimming there could be very dangerous

5 **Maria** I haven't done my homework.
Maria admitted that she hadn't done her homework

6 **Customer** I'll take the smaller model.
Costomer decided to take the smaller model

Reading

1 **a** Read the newspaper article and match the sentence halves.

1 Piers Sharma [e]
2 Mike Ryde [b]
3 Arran Fernandez [a]
4 Francesca [c]
5 Frederick [d]

a took Maths GCSE at the age of five.
b is a college principal.
c is taking a GCSE next year.
d is six years old.
e is waiting for his exam results.

b Read the text again and correct the factual mistakes in these statements.

1 Exam results are coming out later this month. *next month*
2 Piers Sharma got an A* in the exam. *practical*
3 There are five students in Piers' class at school. *nine*
4 The college has a maths course for babies. *computer*
5 Mike Ryde's son is top of the class at school. *daughter*
6 The parents decide when children are ready to take an exam. *Ryde*
7 Mike says the older children love working with computers. *younger*
8 Mike thinks few children could take a GCSE at the age of eleven. *most*

c Match the following words and phrases from the text with the meanings a–j.

1 trepidation [e]
2 momentarily [h]
3 extraordinarily [b]
4 embarked [j]
5 coincidence [a]
6 knock-on effect [d]
7 gravitate [i]
8 horrified [f]
9 dumb down [c]
10 lowest common denominator [g]

a when two things are the same for no reason
b surprisingly
c lower the standard
d causes other things to happen
e slight nervousness or fear
f shocked, frightened
g least difficult thing that everyone understands
h for a very short period of time
i are attracted towards
j began

Who's a clever boy then?

Is it wise for children aged six and seven to be taking GCSE exams, asks Zoe Brennan

Like many youngsters across the country, Piers Sharma will be waiting for the postman with trepidation next month, when exam results come out. Being seven years old, he is not the average GCSE student, however.

'It was a bit hard, and a bit easy,' he says of the exam in computer skills. 'The hard bit was the video conferencing, the applications bit was easy.'

Does he expect to pass? Sharma sounds momentarily stressed. 'I did really well in the practical, I got an A*,' he says. 'In the exam, I might have got a C+ or a B+.'

Most students do their GCSEs at the age of fifteen or sixteen, but Sharma is one of a growing number of pupils sitting exams extraordinarily early. This year, he is one of an entire class of nine children — four seven-year-olds and five six-year-olds — who in May took a GCSE in information and communication technology (ICT) at the private Ryde College in Hertfordshire.

The course takes a year to complete. Mike Ryde, principal of the college, confirmed that three of the children were five years old when they embarked on their GCSE studies, having 'graduated' from the college's baby and toddler computer course, where learning starts at eighteen months. At the age of three or four the infants attend 'primer' lessons. Then Ryde judges when they are ready to sit the exam.

'The most we've ever had before has been one or two children of this age doing a GCSE,' says Ryde. 'The very fact that we've got nine students this year shows that a lot of six and seven-year-olds would be capable of doing this. It is no coincidence that they all started in classes so early.'

The youngest ever to have taken a GCSE at Ryde was Arran Fernandez, who was five when he took Maths in 2001. Ryde's own daughter Francesca, seven, will take the ICT GCSE next year and his son Frederick, six, is on the primer course. 'The wonderful thing is that studying at a level designed for a fifteen-year-old has a knock-on effect,' he says. 'Francesca is topping the class at school.'

'We also have children doing English and Maths really early, but the younger children seem to gravitate towards ICT,' he says. 'They love working with computers.'

Many educationists and parents would be horrified, arguing that six is too young to burden a child with exams. Ryde, however, believes that early GCSEs should be introduced widely, claiming that such a system would reduce the stress on youngsters later on.

'At present, you see children taking upwards of ten GCSES at once at the age of sixteen,' he says. 'That's a tremendous pressure. Why not give them the opportunity to take one or two a year? It seems to me that most children are ready to do a GCSE by the age of eleven. We should not dumb down the system to the lowest common denominator – education is all about opportunity.'

Grammar | *hard* and *hardly*

2 Complete the sentences using the expressions in the box.

> hard (x2)   hardly (x2)
> hardly ever (x2)   hardly anyone (x2)
> hardly anything   hardly anywhere

1 You've _hardly_ touched your food!
2 This is a treat; we _hardly ever_ go to restaurants these days.
3 Although Sam studied _hard_, he wasn't able to pass the test.
4 By ten o'clock there was _hardly anyone_ left in the club.
5 Our teacher _hardly ever_ gives us homework.
6 Monica pushed _hard_ but she couldn't open the door.
7 There's _hardly anyone_ to park in central London.
8 I didn't spend much; I bought _hardly anything_
9 I've _hardly_ seen Isabel since she got married.
10 _hardly anyone_ in my street owns a car.

How to ... | give your opinion

4 Read the dialogue and choose the correct alternative.

Sue: Did you see that item about students on the news? It said that nowadays more than half of them take a year off between school and university. They call it a 'gap year'.

Jake: What do they do?

Sue: They usually go travelling. I (1) *am thinking/think* it's a really good idea.

Jake: I disagree. As far as I'm (2) *concerned/concerning* it's a waste of time.

Sue: Well, I (3) *trust/believe* it can be a very useful experience.

Jake: Why do you think that?

Sue: Well, (4) *for/of* several reasons. (5) *Firstly/First one*, it gets them away from their parents and makes them more independent.

Jake: Getting a job and earning your own money is what makes people independent, (6) *of/in* my opinion.

Sue: That's true. But students on gap years often get jobs while they are travelling (7) *for/because* they need money to live on.

Jake: I thought their parents usually paid for everything.

Sue: Perhaps some of them do, but I don't think that's a very good idea. I mean, if the parents pay for everything, (8) *so/then* their children are never going to become independent.

3 Complete the picture labels using appropriate forms of *hard*, *hardly*, etc. Add any other words that are necessary.

It was very disappointing. _hardly anyone_ came to my barbecue.

Dennis tries really _hard_ but I don't think he'll ever succeed.

I can't help you. I've got _hardly_ any money myself.

I'm not surprised Jane's work is so bad, she _hardly ever_ comes to the class.

I'm afraid there's _hardly anything_ left to eat in the fridge.

We looked _hard_ but we couldn't see where our friend was.

Vocabulary

1 Match the sentence halves.

1 If this product doesn't sell, the company will definitely ☐

2 Deborah's delighted – the book she wrote has become a ☐

3 People don't watch cowboy films any more; I think they've ☐

4 I think you'll have to pull it down and start again; this work really isn't ☐

5 People say that in this life you need a lot of luck in order to ☐

6 We've never done this before but we're willing to ☐

7 After failing the driving test four times, Jim has decided to ☐

8 Nobody bought their new CD; it was a complete ☐

a up to scratch.

b flop.

c succeed.

d best-seller.

e give up.

f go under.

g have a go.

h had their day.

It's time/I'd rather/I'd better

2 Complete each sentence with one word only.

1 It's getting late; I think it's _____ we left.

2 Would you _____ take the bus or the train?

3 Your bedroom's filthy; it's _____ time you tidied up.

4 Look at those dark clouds, you'd _____ take an umbrella.

5 I'm a bit tired; I _____ rather not go out this evening.

6 Don't you think it's about time you _____ your mother – you can use my mobile.

7 She's looking very ill; you _____ better call a doctor.

8 _____ you rather pay me now or wait until next week?

9 You'd better _____ interrupt him right now, he's with a client.

10 I'd rather _____ poor and happy than rich and unhappy.

Vocabulary

3 Choose the correct alternative.

1 My cousin doesn't have unrealistic ideas; he's very down to *ground/earth*.

2 I'm pretty *headstrong/proactive* – I don't take any notice of what other people think.

3 Isabel loves parties; she's very *outgoing/easy-going*.

4 My boss can be very *opinionated/manipulative* so I don't really trust him.

5 You must invite Carol to the party; she's very *high maintenance/witty* and she'll make us all laugh.

6 Everyone takes advantage of David, but then he's a complete *doormat/doorway*.

7 We're looking for a new marketing manager who will be *proactive/open* in developing the business.

8 Like all actors he loves to be the *heart/centre* of attention.

9 Don't be so *selfish/single-minded*; leave some of the chocolate for us.

10 She never listens to reasonable arguments; she's very *opinionated/single-minded*.

4 In seven sentences the adjective in *italics* is incorrect. Tick (✓) the correct sentences then replace the adjectives in the others.

1 Alex was very *devastated* when he heard the news.

2 The children were really *exhausted* after their skiing lesson.

3 Miranda loves cleaning, her kitchen is very *spotless*.

4 My flat is in a great location but it's absolutely *small*.

5 Without the air conditioning our office would get extremely *boiling*.

6 I'm really *hungry*. What's in the fridge?

7 The guided tour of the castle was absolutely *interesting*.

8 It's absolutely *vital* that you take out the correct insurance.

9 Robert was very *ecstatic* about his pay rise.

10 New York can be absolutely *cold* in January.

Reported speech

5 Match the examples of direct speech A–J with the reported speech sentences 1–10. Then complete the sentences.

A Don't touch these plates, they're very hot. ☐

B Where's your passport? ☐

C I'm afraid the doctor's sick today so he can't see you. ☐

D Don't forget to be at the airport two hours before your departure. ☐

E Do all the exercises on page 65 of the Workbook. ☐

F I'll pay back the loan within six months. ☐

G Are you feeling alright, darling? ☐

H Why don't we go to the cinema on Friday evening? ☐

I I stole the money. ☐

J I think I'll have the spaghetti Bolognese. ☐

1 The receptionist explained _____ _____.

2 Our teacher told us _____ _____.

3 My best friend suggested _____ _____.

4 The waitress warned us _____ _____.

5 The criminal admitted _____ _____.

6 The immigration officer asked me _____ _____.

7 My mother asked me _____ _____.

8 The customer decided _____ _____.

9 The travel agent reminded us _____ _____.

10 Elizabeth promised the bank manager _____ _____.

hard and hardly

6 Choose the correct word or phrase to complete the sentences.

1 Since he got married we ___ our son.
   A hardly never see   B hardly ever see
   C hardly are seeing

2 Running the marathon was ___ work.
   A really hard   B hard of   C really hardly

3 If you ___ you can just see the north star above the horizon.
   A hardly look   B look hard   C hard look

4 I can't go out this week, I've got ___ left in my bank account.
   A hardly no money   B hardly money
   C hardly any money

5 Hardly ___ came to the show.
   A nobody   B none   C anyone

6 She ___ but she couldn't reach the top shelf.
   A tried hard   B hardly tried   C hard tried

7 John made one last effort and hit the hammer as ___ as he could.
   A hardly   B hard   C very hardly

8 After the accident I ___ my arm.
   A could hardly move   B could move hardly
   C couldn't hardly move

9 I thought last night's homework was ___.
   A so hardly   B a lot hard   C very hard

10 ___ in this shop is in our price range.
   A Hardly nothing   B Hardly anything
   C Anything hardly

Vocabulary

7 Complete each gap with a word from the box to make expressions with phrasal verbs.

> catch   come   cut   for   get   look
> looking   made   on   put   to (x2)   with (x4)

1 He's my hero. I really _____ up _____ him.

2 If you want to lose weight, you'll have to _____ down _____ all those sweets and cakes!

3 I hear you've got a new car; I'm _____ forward _____ seeing it.

4 Joe's snoring is very irritating – I don't know how you _____ up _____ it.

5 Carol has _____ up _____ a great new idea to make money.

6 They've caught the bank robbers; I'm glad they didn't _____ away _____ it.

7 The runner was slow at first but she _____ up _____ it in the last few metres and won.

8 He's just gone to the shops. You can _____ up _____ him if you run.

H.W ✓

Vocabulary | law and insurance

1 **a** Each sentence contains one word which should be in a different sentence. Find the words and put them in the correct sentences.

1 The judge convicted [*sentenced*] the man to three years in prison.

2 There was a fire at the factory last week; the police think it is fraud. [*arson*]

3 I fell down the steps at work so I sentenced [*sued*] the company and got compensation.

4 You shouldn't use someone else's credit card, that's premium. [*fraud*]

5 I'm glad to say I've never been sued [*convicted*] of any driving offences.

6 The criminal decided to guarantee [*appeal*] against his sentence. [*premium*]

7 The arson [*premium*] on our house insurance seems to get higher every year.

8 We appeal [*guarantee*] all our new cars for three years.

b Complete the sentences.

1 I was shocked when my next-door neighbour was convicted **of** fraud.

2 The injured pedestrian sued the driver **for** €10000.

3 The convicted man was sentenced **to** five years in prison.

4 Each new car is guaranteed **for** three years.

Reading

2 **a** Read the website on page 69 quickly and match the headings with the stories. Three headings are not needed.

A **Fatal Coffee**

B **The Unlucky Car Thief**

C **Imprisoned in a Garage**

D **Nightclub Accident**

E **Don't Ask the Jury**

F **Cruise Control**

b Read the text again and write questions for the following answers.

1 It maintains the vehicle's speed.
What does cruise control do

2 To make himself a cup of coffee.
Why did Mr Grozinski steped on the back of the motorhome

3 A broken arm and leg and cuts to the head.
What injuries did he suffered from

4 To avoid paying the entrance charge.
Why did Kara Walton climbed through the window

5 $12000.
How much did she sued from the owner of the Night club

6 For ten years.
How long Dickson's career as a burglar lasted

7 Because the owners were on vacation.
Why was he tropped in the garage for eight days

8 A supply of dog food and some cans of Pepsi.
What did he used to eat or drink while he was tropped in the garage

c Find the following words and phrases in the text and write them in the correct column. There are five words in each column.

> accelerator awarded broke
> compensation court cruise control
> expenses fell jury knocked out
> mph owner's manual speed starvation
> suffered

Vehicles	Injuries/Harm	Legal
accelerator	suffered	court
cruise control	fell	awarded
speed	broke	compensation
mph	knocked out	expenses
owner's manual	starvation	jury

Compensation Culture or Legal Legends?

1 ___F___ **[A]**

In December 2002 Joseph Grazinski bought a brand-new motor home. He was thrilled because it had cruise control – a switch on the steering wheel which controls the accelerator and maintains the vehicle's speed at a constant rate. A few days after buying the motor home he decided to take it on a trip to Yellowstone National Park. Having joined the motorway, he set the cruise control at 65 mph and decided to step into the back of the motor home to make himself a cup of coffee. Within seconds the motor home had veered off the road, slid down a hillside and turned upside down. Mr Grazinski broke an arm and a leg and suffered cuts to his head.

Mr Grazinski sued the manufacturers because it did not say in the owner's manual that it was dangerous to leave the steering wheel while driving, even if the cruise control was switched on. The court awarded him $175000 and a brand-new motor home.

2 ___D___ **[B]**

In April 1998 Kara Walton of Claymont, Delaware wanted to get into the Black Cat nightclub but she didn't want to pay the $3.50 entrance charge. So she decided to sneak into the club by climbing through the window of the ladies toilet. Unfortunately, while struggling to get through the window she fell to the floor and knocked out her two front teeth.

Ms Walton sued the owner of the Black Cat nightclub and was awarded $12000 compensation plus dental expenses.

3 ___C___ **[C]**

For ten years Terrence Dickson of Bristol, Pennsylvania, had had a successful career as a burglar who specialised in robbing people's houses while they were on holiday. In October 2004 he was about to leave a house he had just robbed when he got stuck in the garage. After entering the garage from the house he realised the door could not be opened from the inside. Because the owners were on vacation he was trapped in the garage for another eight days. During this time he lived on the supply of dog food and some cans of Pepsi which the owners kept at the back of the garage.

Mr Dickson sued the homeowner's insurance company, claiming that he had been the victim of kidnapping, starvation and mental torture. The jury awarded him $500000 compensation.

Grammar | sequencing devices

3 <u>Underline</u> three examples of sentences containing sequencing devices in the text in Ex. 2.

4 Read the sentences and decide which action happened (or started) first, A or B.

1 Having taken two aspirin, I began to feel a little sick.
   A taking two aspirin   B began to feel sick

2 Before going to bed, I have a glass of milk.
   A going to bed   B have a glass of milk

3 After leaving home, he got a job in a circus.
   A leaving home   B got a job in a circus

4 On hearing the news, I rushed out to tell my girlfriend.
   A hearing the news   B rushed out

5 Having crashed his car, Gerry had to come by taxi.
   A coming by taxi   B crashed his car

6 While waiting for the train, I noticed a small child crying on the platform.
   A waiting for the train   B noticed a child

5 Rewrite the sentences using the words in brackets.

Karl took the test then he went out to celebrate. (taken)

Having taken the test, Karl went out to celebrate.

1 Dave told his best friend before he announced the news to his colleagues. (having)
   Having told his best friend Dave announced

2 He got up and went into the village to get some food. (after)
   After getting up he went into the

3 They went to bed after they had watched the midnight movie. (going)
   They watched the midnight movie before going to bed

4 Surinda was watching TV when she heard a strange sound. (while)
   While watching Tv Surinda heard a strange

5 Before we went to the computer shop we read lots of consumer reports. (reading)
   After reading lots of consumer reports we went to the comp

6 Jackie had to get a taxi because she missed the bus. (having)
   Having missed the bus Jackie had to get a taxi

7 My uncle went to America and started a new business. (gone)
   My uncle started a new business after going to America

8 The kids usually do their homework and then watch TV for an hour. (doing)
   The kids usually watch TV for an hour after doing their homework

Grammar | must/might/can't have

1 Match the questions 1–10 with the answers a–h.

1 Why didn't she pass the test? ☐
2 Why did she marry him? ☐
3 Why did she get an A+ in the test? ☐
4 Why did she divorce him? ☐
5 Why didn't she come to work? ☐
6 Why did she do that job? ☐
7 Why didn't she say hello to me? ☐
8 Why was she waving? ☐

a She must have fallen in love.
b She might have been sick.
c She can't have loved him any more.
d She can't have seen you.
e She might have needed the money.
f She can't have done enough revision.
g She must have seen you.
h She must have done lots of work.

2 Rewrite the sentences in *italics* using *must, might* or *can't have*.

1 The plants look very healthy. *Somebody definitely watered them.*

   _____

2 Emma isn't here. *Perhaps she didn't receive the invitation.*

   _____

3 *I'm sure he didn't go out.* I saw the light on in his bedroom.

   _____

4 Their flat is empty. *I'm certain they have left already.*

   _____

5 *I'm sure they haven't left the country.* They don't have passports.

   _____

6 Peter isn't answering his mobile. *Maybe he forgot to take it with him.*

   _____

7 *Maria's probably passed the exam.* She studied very hard.

   _____

8 Where's your umbrella? *I'm absolutely sure you forgot to bring it.*

   _____

3 Complete the text with *must / might / can't have*.

The Mystery of Tutankhamen's Tomb

The discovery of Tutankhamen's tomb is all thanks to one man, Howard Carter. If it hadn't been for Carter's endless curiosity and persistence, the incredible tomb (1) _____ been lost forever. Carter was working in the Valley of the Kings in Egypt when he noticed a pile of ancient rubbish near the entrance of the tomb of Rameses VI. Carter realised that the rubbish (2) _____ been there for a reason and he asked his men to dig into it. Three metres below the original surface they found a stone step carved into the side of the valley. From its depth and position he knew that this step (3) _____ been at least three thousand years old. It turned out to be the first of many steps that led down to the fabulous tomb of Tutankhamen.

It took Carter many months to fully excavate the tomb. But then the archaeologist was left with just as many questions as answers. Who exactly was Tutankhamen and how had he died? From the size of the body he knew that Tutankhamen was only a boy, he (4) _____ been more than eighteen or nineteen when he died. But what killed him? He (5) _____ been murdered by a jealous relative or he (6) _____ died from disease. From the inscriptions in the tomb Carter knew that Tutankhamen (7) _____ come to the throne at the age of about eight or nine. As he died young, he (8) _____ been on the throne for more than about ten years. Yet his tomb was filled with fabulous treasures, worthy of a great king.

Vocabulary | compound adjectives

4 Complete the sentences using compound adjectives. Add any other necessary words.

Damien uses his left hand for writing.

Damien *is left-handed*.

1 Mr Lockwood is fifty years old.
   Mr Lockwood _____.

2 She made the chocolate cake herself.
   The chocolate cake _____.

3 My sister only works for two hours a day.
   My sister _____.

4 It took me weeks and weeks to complete the project.
   The project _____.

5 Elizabeth finds it easy to concentrate and get things done.
   Elizabeth _____.

6 I want a ticket to Hong Kong; I'm not coming back.
   I want a _____.

7 I had a change of mind just before I was due to leave.
   I _____.

8 There's a really modern hospital here; it's just opened.
   There's _____.

Listening

5 a `9.1` Cover the tapescript. Listen to a radio programme and choose the best answers.

1 The radio programme is probably designed for

   A lawyers.   **B** sixteen- to eighteen-year-olds.
   C young children.

2 How many guests will there be on the programme?

   A none   **B** one   **C** more than one

3 Emily says the majority of lawyers work

   A in court.   **B** for criminals.   **C** in offices.

4 Divorce is part of

   A civil law.   **B** criminal law.   **C** court.

5 Emily thinks the most important quality of a barrister is

   A self-confidence.   **B** communication.
   C a good memory.

b Listen again and complete the sentences.

1 There's a factsheet that you can _____ from the website.

2 Emily will help listeners _____ the mysteries of the legal profession.

3 Barristers present a case for the prosecution or _____ the accused.

4 Only a small _____ of lawyers work in court in England.

5 What _____ qualities do you think a good barrister needs?

6 You've got to _____ you know what you're doing.

c Complete the sentences with words and phrases from Ex. 5b.

1 I am writing this letter _____ the board of directors.

2 You're very tanned. You _____ you've been somewhere sunny.

3 I'm going to _____ some MP3 songs from the Internet.

4 This isn't the _____ behaviour I expect from someone like you.

5 Can you help me _____ these cables, they are all jumbled up.

6 You should try to have a large _____ of vegetables in your diet.

TAPESCRIPT

Voice: It's three o'clock and time for this week's edition of *Job Spotlight* with Zack Desmond.

Zack: Hello everyone and welcome once again to *Job Spotlight*. In today's programme we'll be looking at job opportunities in the legal profession. From your letters and emails I know this is a career that a lot of you are considering, so we've also put together a factsheet which you can download from our website. Now, as usual we have several guests here to help us unravel some of the mysteries of this particular profession. My first guest in the studio today is top lawyer Emily Waterstone.

Emily: Hello.

Zack: Welcome to the programme, Emily. Now, you're a barrister, aren't you?

Emily: Yes, a criminal barrister.

Zack: Can you tell us exactly what a barrister does?

Emily: I'll do my best. Actually, I think most people are familiar with barristers from TV and films. We're the people who stand up in court and present the case for the prosecution or on behalf of the accused, that's the person accused of a crime.

Zack: Don't all lawyers do that?

Emily: Not really. In England only a small proportion of lawyers work in court. Most lawyers work in offices – helping people buy houses, make their wills, get divorces – that kind of thing.

Zack: You said you were a criminal barrister. Does that mean you work for criminals?

Emily: No, not exactly. It means I work in criminal law rather than civil law.

Zack: So, what's the difference?

Emily: Well, criminal law is to do with actual crimes – murder, arson, robbery and so on. Civil law isn't about crimes at all; it's the law that governs things like contracts, inheritance, business, things like that.

Zack: So, you wouldn't be able to help me if I wanted to get a divorce.

Emily: I'm afraid not. Well, not unless divorce suddenly became a crime!

Zack: Right. Now for our listeners who are thinking about becoming barristers, what sort of qualities do you think a good barrister needs?

Emily: The main one is self-confidence I think. You've got to look like you know what you're doing. And communication is very important, especially in court.

Zack: I suppose a good understanding of human nature comes in useful.

Emily: Yes, and a good memory helps, too.

Zack: OK. Let's talk about the training you need to do ...

Reading

1 **a** Read the text quickly. Which statement is correct?

1 It summarises the complete plot and characters of *The Hound of the Baskervilles*.

2 It describes Conan Doyle's career using *The Hound of the Baskervilles* as an example.

3 It gives the background to *The Hound of the Baskervilles* and introduces the story.

b Read the text again and decide if the statements are true (T) or false (F).

1 *The Hound of the Baskervilles* was originally a series of magazine stories. ☐

2 People believe that a hound has killed Sir Charles Baskerville. ☐

3 Sir Charles was Henry Baskerville's uncle. ☐

4 Henry Baskerville comes to see Sherlock Holmes. ☐

5 Dr Mortimer is a friend of Sherlock Holmes. ☐

6 Dr Mortimer has some shocking new evidence about the mystery. ☐

7 Sherlock Holmes believes in scientific explanations. ☐

8 Holmes and Watson immediately solve the mystery. ☐

c Find the following words in the text. Decide if they are verbs, nouns or adjectives and match them with the definitions a–h.

1 cliff-hanger ☐   5 heir ☐
2 curse ☐   6 consult ☐
3 beast ☐   7 inquest ☐
4 estate ☐   8 rational ☐

a (*n*) an animal (especially a wild or dangerous animal)

b (*n*) a court case which examines the causes of a person's death

c (*v*) ask for advice from an expert

d (*n*) a promise or legend that something terrible will happen

e (*n*) a large area of land with a house belonging to one person or family

f (*adj*) scientific and logical

g (*n*) an exciting development in a plot that makes the reader want to know more

h (*n*) somebody who inherits land or money when a relative dies

Sherlock Holmes and The Hound of the Baskervilles

(1) *The Hound of the Baskervilles* is one of the most famous and admired detective stories ever written. Published in 1901 and 1902, it originally appeared in nine monthly instalments in *The Strand* magazine. Like Dickens's serialised novels of the same era, each instalment ended with a suspenseful 'cliff-hanger' that kept author Arthur Conan Doyle's audience clamouring for more.

(2) In the story, the old and noble Baskerville family is threatened by a curse: 'A great, black beast, shaped like an enormous wild dog or hound, yet larger than any hound that has ever been seen' terrorises and kills any family member who comes to live at the Baskerville estate. As the story opens, the hound seems to have claimed its latest victim, Sir Charles Baskerville. Sir Charles's nephew, Henry, the new heir to the estate, is about to take up residence the next day. A friend of the family, Dr Mortimer, comes to consult the famous Sherlock Holmes in his rooms at 221b Baker Street, though he admits he doesn't know if the case is more suitable 'for a detective or a priest'. The first instalment of the novel originally ended as Dr Mortimer explains:

(3) '... *One false statement was made by Barrymore at the inquest. He said that there were no traces upon the ground round the body. He did not observe any. But I did – a short distance away, but fresh and clear.'*

'Footprints?'

'Yes, footprints.'

'A man's or a woman's?'

Dr Mortimer looked strangely at us for an instant, and his voice sank almost to a whisper as he answered: 'Mr Holmes, they were the footprints of a gigantic hound!'

(4) Into this atmosphere of ancient secrets, deadly curses and supernatural beasts comes the supremely rational Sherlock Holmes – a man described by his friend Watson as 'the most perfect reasoning and observing machine the world has ever seen'. Piece by piece Holmes and Watson solve the mystery and find the culprit. In the end, they reassure the characters in the novel (as well as Conan Doyle's Victorian readers), that behind the threat of a supernatural 'hound of hell' is a perfectly scientific explanation.

Grammar | relative clauses

2 Match the statements 1 and 2 with the explanations A and B.

1
1 We stayed in the only hotel in the town which had a sea view. ☐
2 We stayed in the only hotel in the town, which had a sea view. ☐
A There were several hotels but only one had a view of the sea.
B There was only one hotel in the town.

2
1 My sister, who lives in Paris, has just had a baby. ☐
2 My sister who lives in Paris has just had a baby. ☐
A I have several sisters and one of them lives in Paris.
B I only have one sister.

3
1 All the students, who can speak French, were invited to the party. ☐
2 All the students who can speak French were invited to the party. ☐
A All of the students were invited to the party.
B Some of the students were invited to the party.

4
1 The cinema, which is opposite the station, is going to become a nightclub. ☐
2 The cinema which is opposite the station is going to become a nightclub. ☐
A There is only one cinema in our town.
B There is more than one cinema in our town.

3 Complete the sentences with relative clauses using the information in the box. Add commas and relative pronouns if necessary.

> We met the girl on holiday.   The hospital is very old.
> It was elected last year.   Her boyfriend lives in Athens.
> ~~She is Spanish.~~   We stayed in the hotel last summer.
> He was Scottish.   I'm living in that house.
> I saw that film yesterday.

John's sister-in-law, *who is Spanish*, is training to be an opera singer.

1 Miranda's boyfriend _____ is a doctor.
2 The house _____ is over a hundred years old.
3 Arthur Conan Doyle _____ was born in 1859.
4 The government _____ has introduced a new tax.
5 Our local hospital _____ is about to be closed down.
6 The girl _____ is coming to stay next weekend.
7 Spielberg's new film _____ was fantastic.
8 The hotel _____ had a heated swimming pool.

Pronunciation

4 **a** 〔9.2〕 The symbol ( ) in these sentences represents the place where we usually pause in normal speech. Are the symbols in the correct place? Listen and check.

1 I bumped into Jane ( ), who used to be married to Steven ( ), last night.
2 I bumped into the girl ( ) who used to be married to Steve.
3 My old friend Steve ( ), who used to be married ( ), was at our school party.

b 〔9.3〕 Mark the pauses in these sentences. In some sentences there may be no pauses. Listen and check.

1 We found our car, which had been towed away two hours earlier, at the police car pound.
2 It was my car that was towed away.
3 The police took the car, which had been blocking someone's gate, to the car pound in Lennard Street.
4 This is the gate that our car was blocking when it was towed away.

Writing

5 Write a short article based on the story in this cartoon strip. Use the guidelines in Ex. 13 on page 126 of the Students' Book to help you.

Vocabulary

1 Use the clues to complete the crossword.

Across

1 The criminal had to pay a ___ of $500.

2 We filed an insurance ___ after our suitcase was stolen.

5 In English courts the ___ wears a wig.

8 £2 million was stolen in the bank ___.

10 The murderer was given a ___ of thirty years in prison.

13 The police found him because he left his ___ on the weapon.

14 My car insurance ___ went up by 20% this year.

Down

1 He's going to ___ a claim with his insurance company.

3 Although she has been convicted, her lawyer is going to make an ___ to a higher court.

4 After the car crash we had to ___ the other driver for compensation.

6 The DVD player comes with a 12-month ___ from the manufacturers.

7 The pictures from the shop's cameras helped to ___ the shoplifter.

9 The ___ stole my handbag while I was dancing.

11 That wasn't an accidental fire, it was ___.

12 Credit card ___ is one of the fastest-growing crimes.

Sequencing devices

2 Choose the correct alternative.

1 Before *leaving/left* the meeting, she handed me her business card.

2 Having *seeing/seen* the film myself, I wouldn't recommend it.

3 *At/On* arriving at the airport the tourist group were met by the travel agent.

4 *After/Before* taking the tablets I felt a lot better – they were very effective.

5 Having opened the door, she *runs/ran* into the garden.

6 Before *booking/booked* the holiday, we did a lot of research.

7 While *lived/living* in New York, Kirsten made many new friends.

8 *To have/Having* taken the express train, Derek arrived in plenty of time.

9 On *the finish/finishing* his speech, the politician got a round of applause.

10 Having *learned/being learned* Spanish at school, the children were able to communicate during their holiday.

must/might/can't have

3 Read the situation and complete the sentences using appropriate forms of *must/might/can't have*.

Last night £50,000 was stolen from the safe of Western United Bank. None of the doors or locks was broken so the police think somebody working in the bank stole the money. There were no fingerprints on the safe door, but the police found a cigarette end on the floor near the safe. Nobody is allowed to smoke in the bank. Only three members of staff have keys to the safe: Mr Briggs the manager, Jennifer the assistant manager and Darren, the chief cashier. Mr Briggs was at home with his wife all last night. His wife confirms this. Jennifer says she was at home, but she lives alone. Darren says he was at home. He lives with his parents. His mother says he was at home all night, except when he went outside to take the dog for a walk at midnight.

1 The money _____ been stolen by a member of staff because none of the doors or locks was broken.

2 It _____ been either Mr Briggs, Jennifer or Darren because they are the only ones with keys to the safe.

3 The thief _____ been a smoker because there was a cigarette end on the floor.

4 It _____ been Mr Briggs because he was at home with his wife all night.

5 Jennifer _____ stolen the money because she can't prove she was at home last night.

6 Darren _____ stolen the money when he went out for a walk at midnight.

Vocabulary

4 Complete the sentences with compound adjectives. The first letter of each adjective is given.

1 This cake is delicious, is it h_____?

2 I never buy second-hand things, I like everything to be b_____.

3 Yes, sir. A first class ticket to Glasgow – o_____ or return?

4 I'm afraid we only have p_____ jobs available at the moment.

5 You can tell from her writing that she's l_____.

6 It was a l_____ decision to come here because we didn't know our holiday dates until last week.

7 I find filling in my tax form incredibly t_____.

8 She's really determined and s_____ about getting what she wants.

9 Car insurance is much cheaper for m_____ people than for youngsters.

10 I really wouldn't trust that s_____ friend of yours; she's quite dishonest.

Relative clauses

5 Six sentences contain mistakes with grammar and punctuation. Rewrite the incorrect sentences. Add relative pronouns and commas where necessary.

1 My brother that works in Cardiff is an opera singer.

2 Jenny of who I told you about last week is getting married.

3 The house we saw last weekend is worth over £1 million.

4 The children didn't pass the test had to take it again.

5 Our car which, we bought last year has been stolen, from our garage.

6 The film was on TV last night was absolutely fascinating.

7 Pilar, who guided us around the town, is a real expert on Spanish history.

8 My colleague, which showed us how to use the computer has been promoted, to the Los Angeles office.

6 Use defining and non-defining relative clauses to make each numbered pair of sentences into one sentence. The first one has been done as an example.

1 The house has been sold. It is the house where I used to play as a child.

2 It belonged to an old lady. The old lady died.

3 When I was young the old lady allowed me to play in her garden. The old lady used to be a schoolteacher.

4 The garden had lots of lemon trees. The garden was huge.

5 I used to pick the lemons from the trees. The trees grew there.

6 The old lady used the lemons to make lemonade. I had picked the lemons.

1 *The house where I used to play as a child has been sold.*

2 _____

3 _____

4 _____

5 _____

6 _____

Vocabulary

7 Read the newspaper headlines and decide if the statements are true (T) or false (F).

Manchester United bids for top Portuguese player

BBC to axe top comedy show

Ministers clash over immigration

French Actress quits Hollywood

Prime Minister backs strikers

CHILDREN RESCUED FROM HOTEL BLAZE

Oscar-winning director in divorce drama

Government aid for homeless rises 25%

1 Manchester United has bought a Portuguese football player. ☐

2 The BBC will cancel a popular comedy show. ☐

3 Government ministers disagree about immigration. ☐

4 A French actress has left Hollywood. ☐

5 The Prime Minister wants the strikers to go back to work. ☐

6 Firefighters have rescued some children from a hotel fire. ☐

7 An award-winning director is making a film about a divorce. ☐

8 The Government says a quarter of homeless people have a disease. ☐

Listening

1 **a** [10.1] Cover the tapescript. Listen to the extract from a radio programme and choose the best summary.

1 The extract is a book review.
2 The extract is an interview with a writer.
3 The extract is about a famous French hypnotist.

b Listen again and use the information to complete the notes on Franz Mesmer's life. Write one word or number in each gap.

1734	• born in (1) _____
1766	• (2) _____ as a doctor from (3) _____ university • started using (4) _____ on sick patients
1777	• moved to (5) _____. • became famous treating French (6) _____, he even treated the (7) _____. • he cured people but he also (8) _____ them.
1785	• he was (9) _____ to go back to Germany.
(10) _____	• he died

c Match the words and phrases 1–8 with the things they refer to A–D. Then listen again or read the tapescript to check your answers.

1 quite unique ☐
2 a kind of magic ☐
3 a great showman ☐
4 a recently discovered phenomenon ☐
5 were treated by Mesmer ☐
6 surprisingly effective ☐
7 like theatrical displays ☐
8 gullible ☐

A Franz Anton Mesmer
B Mesmer's treatments of patients
C French aristocrats
D magnetism

TAPESCRIPT

I: This week's biography choice is *Mesmer – The Original Hypnotist*. It is the story of Franz Anton Mesmer, the 18th-century scientist who is often regarded as the founder of hypnotism. With me in the studio is its author, Alexander Bond. Alexander, can I start by asking you what attracted you to this character?

B: Yes. Well, I've always been interested in hypnotists and I wanted to find out how hypnotism first started, so obviously that led me to Franz Mesmer.

I: Now, Mesmer is quite unique, isn't he?

B: Yes. He's one of the very few people whose name has become an English verb.

I: As in 'to be mesmerised by something' ...

B: Exactly. And that shows just how influential and important he was.

I: He was French, wasn't he?

B: Actually he was born in Germany, in 1734. And he studied medicine in Austria – at the university of Vienna, in fact.

I: So how did he first became famous?

B: Well, after he qualified as a doctor in 1766 he started doing experiments with magnets. Magnetism was a recently discovered phenomenon but it wasn't properly understood. People saw metal objects flying towards each other and it seemed to be a kind of magic. Anyway, Mesmer started applying magnets to his sick patients ...

I: To sick people?

B: Yes. In fact, it was surprisingly effective. Lots of his patients got better and Mesmer soon became the best-known doctor in Vienna. But the other doctors resented his success and forced him to move to Paris in 1777.

I: And that's where he became really famous?

B: Yes. Paris was pretty much the centre of European culture at the time, and the French were fascinated by Mesmer and his magnetic cures. Many members of the French aristocracy were treated by him. Even King Louis XVI became one of his patients. But then Mesmer was a great showman, his treatments were more like theatrical displays, so as well as curing people he entertained them.

I: But how did it work?

B: Well, we think that what he was really doing was hypnotising people. From detailed descriptions written at the time it seems he probably used the power of hypnotism to convince his patients they were feeling better.

I: He must have made a lot of money from those gullible French aristocrats!

B: Yes, he made a fortune. But his success didn't last for long. He failed to cure some influential members of French society and in 1785 he was forced to go back to Germany.

I: Did he carry on his medical work there?

B: Not really. But he had a happy and contented retirement. And he lived until 1815.

Vocabulary | belief and opinion

2 There is one unnecessary or incorrect word in each sentence. Correct the mistakes.

1 Are you in favour that the law against smoking in restaurants?

2 I'm quite sceptic that anyone can read another person's mind.

3 My friend is reckons that there are ghosts in his house.

4 He's convenienced that the government is lying to us.

5 The police suspect of the murderer knew the victim.

6 I'm against give money to beggars.

Grammar | reflexive pronouns

3 Complete the sentences with the correct words.

1 They've got an oven that cleans ___.
 A himself B itself C them

2 Our teacher told ___ to do exercise 3.
 A ourselves B we C us

3 Successful team work depends on people helping ___.
 A each other   B ourself
 C each others

4 When he went on holiday David took his computer with ___.
 A itself B himself C him

5 I hurt ___ when I was lifting a heavy suitcase.
 A myself B me C my

6 Emma sat down and relaxed ___ twenty minutes.
 A her for B herself for C for

7 The children really enjoyed ___ on the rollercoaster.
 A themselves B itself C each other

8 We couldn't afford builders so we decided to build the house ___.
 A myself B each other C ourselves

9 It's very important to concentrate ___ you are driving.
 A while B yourself while
 C yourselves

10 At the end of the presentations I want you to give ___ marks out of ten.
 A themselves   B each other C you

4 Rewrite the sentences using reflexive pronouns or *each other*.

Janna looked at her reflection in the mirror.
Janna looked at herself in the mirror.

1 Darren cut his hand while he was gardening.
 _____

2 I made the cake without anyone's help.
 _____

3 We've made all the arrangements; nobody helped us.
 _____

4 Mandy sent a text message to Sylvia and Sylvia sent one to Mandy.
 _____

5 My central heating turns on automatically if the temperature drops.
 _____

6 The Bensons often send packages to their home address when they are abroad.
 _____

7 Did you paint this picture on your own?
 _____

8 Isabel doesn't work for anybody else; she's self-employed.
 _____

How to ... | ask about other people's views

5 Put the words in the correct order to make questions. Then answer the questions with your own opinions.

1 about do you strong feelings have pollution any ?
 _____?

2 poverty feel how about do you
 _____?

3 the for are death penalty you or against
 _____?

4 on what fast food are views your
 _____?

5 think divorce of what do you
 _____?

Reading

1 a Read the newspaper article quickly and choose the best summary.

1 Artificial smells haven't lived up to expectations.

2 Artificial smells have huge potential for business.

3 Banks hope artificial smells will increase their profits.

b Read the text again and decide if the following statements are true (T) or false (F).

1 Dale Air has produced an artificial 'smell of money' for Barclays Bank. ☐

2 The bank is having problems with its air conditioning systems. ☐

3 It is difficult to isolate the real smell of money. ☐

4 Shoppers are aware of the effect smells have on their spending. ☐

5 The smell of coconuts seems to encourage people to buy holidays. ☐

6 Cafés often put coffee machines near the entrance. ☐

7 The human sense of smell is highly developed. ☐

8 Most of the scientific problems of producing artificial smells have now been solved. ☐

c Find the following words and phrases in the text.

1 a compound adjective to describe bread which has just been made _____

2 an adjective meaning the opposite of *pessimistic* _____

3 a phrasal verb which means *to collect or attract something* _____

4 a compound noun that describes a machine used to store money in a shop _____

5 an adverb we use when something is done in a clever and almost invisible way _____

6 a scientific phrase which describes the parts of the body we smell things with _____

7 an adjective made from the verb *to evoke* _____

8 a verb which means *to control something and use it for your own benefit* _____

The Smell of Money

1

For many years large supermarkets have been encouraging us to spend money by pumping the smell of freshly-baked bread into their stores. Now Dale Air, a leading firm of aroma consultants, has been approached by Barclay's Bank to develop suitable artificial smells for their banks. Researchers have suggested that surrounding customers with the 'smell of money' will encourage them to feel relaxed and optimistic and give them added confidence in the bank's security and professionalism.

2

But before a smell can be manufactured and introduced into banks' air conditioning systems it must be identified and chemically analysed, and this has proved to be difficult. The problem is that banknotes and coins tend to pick up the smell of their surroundings. So cash that has been sitting in a cash register at a fishmonger's will smell of fish, and banknotes used to pay for meals in restaurants will tend to smell of food.

3

It may be a challenge, but aroma experts have little doubt that the use of artificial smells can be an effective form of subconscious advertising. Lunn Poly, a British travel company, introduced the smell of coconuts into its travel agencies and saw a big increase in spending by holiday makers. Many cafés now have electric dispensers that release the smell of freshly roasted coffee near their entrances, subtly encouraging customers to come in and have a drink or snack. Even prestige car maker Rolls-Royce has been spraying the inside of its cars to enhance the smell of the leather seats.

4

'The sense of smell is probably the most basic and primitive of all human senses,' explains researcher Jim O'Riordan. 'There is a direct pathway from the olfactory organs in the nose to the brain.' It is certainly true that most people find certain smells incredibly evocative, stirring memories and feelings in a way that few other stimulants can rival. It is a phenomenon marketing consultants have long recognised, but until recently have been unable to harness. 'We've made great progress but the technology of odour production is still in its infancy,' says O'Riordan. 'Who knows where it will take us.'

Vocabulary | advertising

2 Label the texts/words 1–4 using the following words (not all the words are needed):

publicity   makes   advertisement
classified ad   marketing   target market
slogan

'You deserve the best'

1 _____

Siemens

Sony

Boeing

Rolls-Royce

For Sale
2003 Toyota Corrolla
40,000 miles
Excellent condition.
£3,000
Tel 03303778899

2 _____

3 _____

Married women living in the
United States between the
ages of 30 and 45 with annual
incomes in excess of $25,000.

4 _____

Pronunciation

3 **10.2** How many syllables do these words have? Put the words into the correct column and mark the main stress on each word. Then listen and check.

advertisement   commercial   customers
information   magazines   persuasion
politicians   supermarket

Three syllables	Four syllables

Grammar | gerunds and infinitives

4 Choose the correct alternative.

1 Did your colleagues *refuse/suggest* working at the weekends?
2 The boss suggested *join/joining* her for lunch.
3 Let me know when you've finished *writing/to write* the report.
4 He encouraged *her to get/to get her* a new job.
5 Could you *promise/imagine* living without a mobile phone?
6 Sheila should practise *speaking/to speak* Spanish before she goes to Madrid.
7 Will you *miss/agree* playing football on Saturdays?
8 Did you persuade her *coming/to come*?

5 Match the sentence halves.

1   1 I stopped watching TV ☐
    2 I stopped to watch TV ☐
    A and answered the phone.
    B because there was a fascinating documentary on.

2   1 I regret to say ☐
    2 I regret saying ☐
    A you were lazy, it was very rude of me.
    B that you have not been selected for the team.

3   1 I remember locking the door before ☐
    2 Remember to lock the door before ☐
    A you go home.
    B I left.

4   1 Hilary tried closing the door but ☐
    2 Hilary tried to close the door but ☐
    A there was still a cold draught in the room.
    B it was jammed and she couldn't do it.

Writing

6 Look at your answers in Ex. 5 on page 77. Write an essay, using one of these titles.

- Pollution is the most serious threat facing the modern world.
- The death penalty should be used for all convicted murderers.
- Fast food is dangerous to people's health and should be banned completely.

Look at the guidelines in Ex. 11 on page 137 of the Students' Book to help you.

Reading

1 **a** Read the text quickly and choose the best heading for each paragraph. Two of the headings are not needed.

A Subconscious Suggestion

B The Future

C Advertising

D Fiction or Reality?

E Pavlov

F New Drugs

G Conditioning and Indoctrination

b Read the text again and write questions for the answers.

1 _____?

Memories of a failed romance.

2 _____?

Changes in brain chemistry.

3 _____?

More than forty.

4 _____?

Through subtle suggestion and manipulation

5 _____?

By endlessly repeating tasks and sequences.

6 _____?

Which parts of the brain control individual movements.

c Find words or phrases in the text that mean:

1 something invented/not true (*n*, para 1)
_____

2 people who study the brain (*n*, para 2)
_____

3 chemicals made from several different ingredients (*n*, para 2) _____

4 take away/remove (*v*, para 2) _____

5 surprised/impressed (*-ed adj*, para 3)
_____

6 getting people to do what you want by secretly tricking them (*n*, para 3)
_____

7 instructions given to you by a superior (*n*, para 4) _____

8 do a task (*phrasal v*, para 4) _____

9 distorted information given to people by a government or organisation to influence them (*n*, para 4) _____

10 sudden desire or wish (*n*, para 5)
_____

Mind Control – is it real?

1

With the release of *Eternal Sunshine of the Spotless Mind* the subject of mind control is once again in the news. In the film Joel has bad memories of a failed romance removed from his mind by the sinister Lacuna organisation. Of course, the film is only fiction. But could such a thing happen in real life?

2

Scientists point to the recent development of several drugs which appear to influence the brain. Known as memory-management drugs, these new compounds can cause changes in brain chemistry, and seem to directly influence the part of the brain that stores and processes past experiences. Neuroscientists hope to make products which can improve memory skills and even erase negative thoughts. The American Food and Drug Administration (FDA) is testing more than forty such products.

3

Drugs are not the only way the mind can be controlled. Viewers of Channel 4's series on mind control featuring Derren Brown have been amazed at how he can put ideas into people's minds through subtle suggestion and manipulation. Similar effects are achieved by hypnotists, although they always claim they are only harnessing the mind's own hidden desires and wishes. Some even claim that advertisements include invisible triggers that stimulate the subconscious to make us want particular products.

4

More traditional forms of mind control are well-known. For centuries armies have been training soldiers to obey orders without thinking using a method now known as Pavlovian conditioning, named after Russian psychologist Ivan Pavlov. By endlessly repeating tasks and sequences and by employing simple tactics of punishment and reward, people can be persuaded to carry out instructions without question. On a larger scale the technique of indoctrination can be employed. Through the use of education and propaganda, dictators and governments throughout history have convinced people of things which are obviously untrue.

5

The future holds even more worrying possibilities. Research has shown us exactly which parts of the brain control individual movements. Once we have learned how to stimulate these areas we will be able to make people move in whichever way we want. The concept of a human robot, its mind and body obedient to another person's every whim, has become a distinct possibility.

Vocabulary | speaking

2 Complete the crossword using the clues below.

Across

1 Please ___; I don't want anyone else to hear us.
4 You should speak more clearly – don't ___.
5 I'm afraid I ___ whenever I see a spider.
7 The news was so shocking I was ___ for words.
8 She's never afraid to speak her ___.

Down

2 Please don't ___ me when I'm in the middle of telling a joke.
3 I can't keep a secret; I ___ things out at the worse times!
6 Excuse me. Can I have a ___ with you about this invoice?

Grammar | *If* structures (2)

3 a Match the sentence halves to make correct conditional sentences.

***If* clause**

1 If we hadn't missed the plane, ☐
2 If you don't like Coldplay, ☐
3 Provided you pay for the tickets, ☐
4 If I had plenty of money, ☐
5 If we'd gone to the concert, ☐
6 As long as I work overtime, ☐
7 Unless you pay for it, ☐
8 If we hadn't managed to get tickets, ☐

Main clause

a I'd take a six-month holiday.
b we wouldn't have seen Coldplay.
c we would be on holiday now.
d I'll go to the concert with you.
e I can have an extra week's holiday.
f you shouldn't have bought tickets for their show.
g we would have seen the band.
h I won't go to the concert with you.

b Answer these questions about the completed sentences in Ex. 3a.

1 Is sentence 1 3rd Conditional or Mixed Conditional?
2 Is sentence 6 Zero Conditional or 1st Conditional?
3 Is sentence 5 3rd Conditional or Mixed Conditional?
4 Which type of conditional is sentence 4?
5 Which type of conditional is sentence 2?

4 Complete the second sentence so that it means the same as the first.

You can put on the life jacket, but only if there is an emergency.
Don't put on the life jacket *unless there is an emergency.*

1 We went to the sales and bought an incredibly cheap sofa.
   If we hadn't gone _____
   _____.

2 Charles forgot to turn on his alarm clock so he overslept.
   Charles wouldn't have overslept _____
   _____.

3 Plants grow when you give them water.
   If you _____
   _____.

4 One day I might get a pay rise and then I'll be able to buy a nice house.
   If I got a pay rise _____
   _____.

5 Only use the generator if there is a power failure.
   Don't use the generator _____
   _____.

6 We will give you a guarantee if you pay by credit card.
   Provided _____
   _____.

7 If the neighbours complain, you can't have a party.
   You can have a party _____
   _____.

8 If you show us a receipt, we can give you a refund.
   As long as _____
   _____.

Vocabulary

1 Choose the correct alternative.

1 Harold was knocked *subconscious/unconscious* by the falling tree.

2 Although I had never been there before I had a strong feeling of *sixth sense/déjà vu*.

3 I always *trust/believe* my intuition about new people I meet.

4 Before we left for the airport I had an awful *premonition/intuition* that something bad was about to happen.

5 It isn't really difficult to learn new skills; it's just a question of *brain/mind* over matter.

6 You need a lot of *premonition/willpower* to give up smoking.

7 My brother gets very stressed about his work; I think he has a *subconscious/unconscious* fear of failure.

8 Hypnotists are experts at using the power of *persuasion/intuition*.

Reflexive pronouns

2 Six of the sentences contain mistakes with pronouns. Find the mistakes and correct them.

1 Emma cut her while doing the washing up.

2 Mike takes his laptop with himself when he goes on business trips.

3 Juanita and Mario phone each others every day.

4 I'm going to teach myself to play the violin.

5 To save money we painted our house ourself.

6 Mr and Mrs Wright decided to take their grandchildren with themselves when they went on holiday.

7 I have no objections to the product itself; it's the advertisement that annoys me.

8 I repaired me the broken chair.

Vocabulary

3 Rewrite the sentences using suitable forms of the phrases in the box. Use each phrase once only.

> to have always believed that   to be against
> to be sceptical about   to be convinced
> ~~to have your doubts about~~   reckon   to be in favour of

Janet isn't really sure about this new job.
Janet has her doubts about this new job.

1 I am absolutely certain that Jimmy is guilty of the crime.

_____

2 Emily supports the idea of longer prison sentences for criminals.

_____

3 I think she could be our new manager.

_____

4 All my life I have had the opinion that people are basically honest.

_____

5 Some politicians don't support the new tax.

_____

6 I really don't completely trust or believe in hypnosis.

_____

4 Use the clues to complete the crossword.

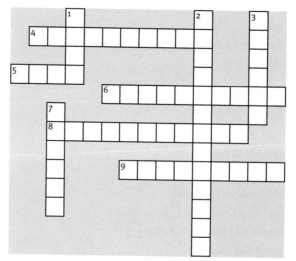

Across

4 A small advertisement in a newspaper is a ___ ad.

5 Publicity that makes something seem important.

6 A ___ break is a series of advertisements between TV programmes.

8 A noun made from the verb *to advertise*.

9 Deciding where and how to sell products, how much to charge, etc.

Down

1 What ___ is it? Sony or Philips?

2 Pictures/Words/Short film that tries to sell you a product.

3 A short clever phrase used by advertisers or politicians.

7 For this product our target ___ is teenagers.

Gerunds and infinitives

5 Complete the sentences using appropriate forms of the words in brackets.

1 Jane's father agreed _____ from the nightclub. (collect/us)

2 Did you remember _____ before you left? (turn on/the burglar alarm)

3 Have you considered _____ in other countries? (apply/to universities)

4 We regret _____ that your job application has been unsuccessful. (inform/you)

5 My grandfather carried on _____ until he was 80. (work/as a doctor)

6 It was an expensive city but we enjoyed _____. (live/there)

7 I would avoid _____ – they taste disgusting. (eat/the prawns)

8 It was a very long drive so at one o'clock I stopped _____. (have/lunch)

9 Her new job involves _____ and publicity materials. (design/websites)

10 My teacher persuaded _____ the first certificate exam next summer. (me/take)

Vocabulary

6 Match the descriptions 1–6 with the phrases a–h. Two of the phrases are not needed.

1 When you speak quietly because you only want one person to hear you. ☐

2 When you can't think what to say. ☐

3 When you tell people exactly what you think about something, even if it is shocking. ☐

4 When you say something quickly without thinking about it. ☐

5 When you speak quietly and not very clearly. ☐

6 When you say something while another person is still speaking. ☐

a to be lost for words

b to shriek

c to interrupt

d to whisper

e to have a word with

f to mumble

g to blurt out

h to speak your mind

If structures (2)

7 Complete the sentences with the correct words.

1 I'll go to the party ___ you agree to come with me.
   A unless   B as long as   C if not

2 If we ___ stuck in this traffic jam, we would be there by now.
   A didn't get   B don't get   C hadn't got

3 If the film hadn't ended so late, we ___ the last bus home.
   A would miss   B wouldn't have missed   C don't miss

4 We'll give you a refund ___ back the receipt.
   A provided you bring   B provided you brought
   C unless you bring

5 If she isn't at home, ___ the invitation through the letter box.
   A you would put   B put   C you have put

6 If I ___ to a part-time job, I'd have a lot more time with the children.
   A changed   B will change   C had changed

7 If you've lived there all your life, you ___ how beautiful it is.
   A will already know   B had already known
   C already knew

8 If we'd arrived earlier, we ___ the film stars arriving.
   A might see   B saw   C might have seen

9 You mustn't use that expensive mobile phone ___ it's a real emergency.
   A if   B provided   C unless

10 Darren ___ in the winning team if he hadn't broken his leg.
   A wasn't   B could have been   C can be

Vocabulary

8 Match the letters in the box with the gaps in the words. Each gap may be two or three letters long.

> cc   ea   ei   el   ell   il   iou   ou   ss   syc

1 int___igence

2 p___hologist

3 subconsc___s

4 th___r

5 responsib___ity

6 definit___y

7 chang___ble

8 nece___ary

9 gener___s

10 o___asionally

Unit 1 People

Lesson 1.1
Reading

1a **1** D **2** E **3** A **4** C **5** B

b **1** No. **2** Yes. **3** Marta Kauffman and David Crane.
4 Because they are believable and almost everybody can
identify with them. **5** The interaction between the contrasting
personalities. **6** They seemed to live lives of endless leisure
in unfeasibly large apartments although they had very ordinary
jobs. **7** By bringing in new characters and guest stars.
8 The focus on the six main characters.

c **1** profitable **2** nominated **3** equivalent **4** ratings
5 network **6** tuned in **7** command **8** endearing **9** bond
10 run out of steam

Writing

2a **1** C **2** B **3** A

b

1
> Bill
> Thanks for agreeing to feed ~~the~~ cats!
> ~~The~~ cat food is on ~~the~~ top shelf in ~~the~~ cupboard.
> ~~And~~ don't forget to give them ~~some~~ water.
> ~~I'm~~ back ~~on~~ Thursday.
> Jerry

2
> Party tonight ~~at~~ 9 p.m.
> ~~The~~ garden flat at 82 Mandeville Road.
> ~~It is~~ just behind a big Supersaver supermarket.
> Bring ~~some nice~~ food!
> Millie X X

3
> Darren
> Harriet from ~~the~~ Accounts ~~Department~~ called ~~at~~ 3 o'clock.
> Please email her ~~the~~ figures for ~~the~~ Smithson account before
> tomorrow morning.
> ~~Her~~ email ~~is~~ harriet.donald@smiths.org.ur
> Tricia

Grammar: question tags

3 **1** shouldn't we? **2** could he? **3** do they? **4** shall we?
5 didn't you? **6** does it? **7** will you? **8** did they? **9** won't you?
10 aren't I?

4 **1** Nobody likes cabbage, ~~does he?~~ do they? **2** ✓
3 You can't use a mobile phone on the plane, ~~can't you?~~ can you?
4 Somebody told you, ~~didn't he?~~ didn't they? **5** ✓ **6** Hilary isn't
married, ~~isn't she?~~ is she? **7** Nothing's expensive in this shop, ~~are~~
~~they?~~ is it? **8** ✓

Pronunciation

5a **1** R **2** R **3** R **4** F **5** R **6** F **7** R **8** R **9** F **10** R
b **1** B **2** D **3** B **4** A **5** D **6** A **7** C **8** B **9** A **10** C

Lesson 1.2
Listening

1a 3

b **1** T **2** T **3** F **4** F **5** F **6** T **7** T **8** F

c **1** author **2** tossing **3** tomb **4** swords **5** confined
6 grave stone **7** myths **8** linked

Grammar: any/every/no/some

2 **1** only **2** nothing **3** all **4** everybody **5** Anybody
6 everything **7** somebody **8** anything **9** some **10** something

3 **1** Nobody won any prizes. **2** Would you like some/any water?
3 We've been through everything and we can't find your application
form. **4** I'm sorry but we haven't got anything available in July.
5 Everyone in my street own cars. **6** I waited at reception for ages
but I couldn't find anybody to help me. **7** We've got lots of silk
dresses but I'm afraid we have none/nothing in your size.
8 Jane always has some flowers in her flat.

Vocabulary: making adjectives from nouns

4 **1** artistic **2** responsible **3** skill **4** importance
5 successful **6** lonely **7** frustrated **8** intellect

How to: agree/disagree

5 **1** c **2** f **3** e **4** a **5** d **6** b

Lesson 1.3
Listening

1a **1** C **2** A **3** D **4** B

b **1** The man *mainly* uses his phone to send text messages.
2 He's *can't* use his phone at work. **3** The man expects train
journeys to be *peaceful and quiet.* **4** The woman thinks it's
cheap/not expensive to make mobile phone calls. **5** Steve's
mobile was *a bargain/cheap.* **6** John *thinks Steve's new phone is
sophisticated.* **7** The customer *has* children. **8** If he isn't happy
after 10 days the customer can get *a refund.*

c **1** e **2** h **3** f **4** i **5** g **6** a **7** c **8** j **9** d **10** b

Vocabulary: noises

2 **1** bark **2** screamed **3** ring **4** creak **5** banged **6** thud

Grammar: present/future modals of possibility

3 **1** b **2** e **3** f **4** a **5** c **6** d
4 **1** B **2** A **3** B **4** A **5** A **6** C **7** B **8** A **9** A **10** C

Review and consolidation unit 1

Vocabulary

1

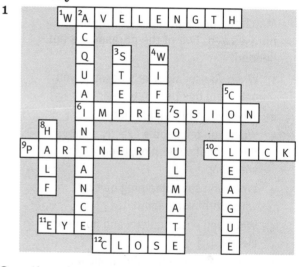

Questions tags

2 **1** haven't they **2** aren't **3** shall **4** couldn't
5 does **6** Something **7** do **8** won't

any/every/no/some

3 **1** A✓ B✗ **2** A✓ B✓ **3** A✗ B✓ **4** A✗ B✗ **5** A✓ B✓
6 A✗ B✓ **7** A✓ B✗ **8** A✗ B✓

Vocabulary

4 **1** lonely **2** intellectual **3** artistic **4** skill **5** successful
6 responsibility **7** jealous **8** important

5 **1** snoring **2** screamed **3** bark **4** creaks **5** bang **6** ring

Present/Future modals of possibility

6 **1** B **2** A **3** B **4** C **5** B **6** B **7** C **8** B **9** A **10** C

Vocabulary

7 **1** gets on **2** looked up to **3** Bringing up **4** have split up
5 show off **6** takes after **7** have/'ve fallen out
8 is/'s going out with

Unit 2 Work

Lesson 2.1
Listening

1a **1** actor **2** photographer **3** hotel receptionist **4** architect

b **1** show off (b) **2** buzz (g) **3** line of work (e)
4 snowballed (d) **5** freelance (h) **6** a real handful (a)
7 a thing for (c) **8** in the blood (f)

c **1** 'm appearing **2** 'll take **3** 'll be leaving **4** are going to live

Vocabulary: verb phrases about work

2 **1** is able to meet tight deadlines **2** gets the best out of
other people **3** keeps calm under pressure **4** is good with
figures **5** does voluntary work **6** has a 'can do' attitude
7 works well in a team **8** took early retirement **9** is good at using
her own initiative **10** has been promoted

Grammar: futures overview

3 **1** 'll try **2** 're going to see **3** is starting **4** don't think I'll
have **5** 'll probably come **6** is opening **7** is going to be
8 's bound **9** 'm attending **10** will definitely be/is definitely
going to be

How to: talk about future plans

4 **1** I've decided I'm going to start doing some exercise.
2 I'm not sure about buying that jacket. **3** I'm planning to have
a lie-in on Sunday. **4** I'm bound to get married one day.
5 I probably won't win the lottery. **6** I'd like to have a holiday.

Lesson 2.2
Reading

1a **1** It refers to the feelings people should have about the shocking
amount of waste in modern society. **2** It is significant because it
weighs the same as the amount of electrical equipment thrown away
by an average person in a lifetime. **3** It ends up in landfill sites or is
incinerated.

b (Any two of the following)

Adjectives: shocking, extravagant, assorted, surprising, average,
sheer, electronic

Adverbs: dramatically, unnecessarily, currently

Parts of the human body: teeth , eyes, ears

Electronic equipment: televisions, mobile phones, satellite dishes,
computer mice

Domestic appliances: washing machines, fridges, vacuum cleaners,
kettles, microwaves

c **1** discarded **2** commissioned **3** extravagant
4 high-tech **5** cabling **6** mice **7** encourage **8** currently
9 landfill sites **10** incinerated

Grammar: Future Perfect and Future Continuous

2 **1** No, I'll be going in August instead. **2** Yes, he should
have finished it by then. **3** No, I'm afraid he'll be seeing
another client then. **4** Yes, we should have received planning
permission by then. **5** Yes, they will be staying with us from
July to September. **6** No, I'll be working at home all day
tomorrow. **7** Pretty well. By the end of next month we should have
finished most of it. **8** Yes, she will have done it by lunchtime at the
latest.

3 **1** will have finished **2** will have left **3** 'll be lying
4 'll be bringing **5** will have arrived

Pronunciation

4a The pronunciation is different.

b **1** A **2** B **3** A **4** B **5** B

Vocabulary: 'after work' activities

5 **1** ~~social~~ socialise **2** ~~make~~ do **3** ~~for~~ with **4** ✓
5 ✓ **6** ~~day~~ date

Lesson 2.3
Reading

1a **A** shift work (n) **B** work force (n) **C** work out (phr v)
D workaholic (adj) **E** working on (phr v) **F** working class (n)

b **1** work on something **2** work ethic **3** work out
4 work-shy **5** workaholic **6** work force **7** work load
8 working class **9** shift work **10** workmanship **11** work permit
12 work station

Grammar: in case

2 **1** Maria took plenty of toys in case the children got
bored. **2** We're going to get extra copies of the keys made in case
we lose one. **3** Please listen for the doorbell in case they deliver the
parcel this morning. **4** Leave your mobile turned on in case I need
to contact you. **5** I took some sandwiches in case the food on the
train was too expensive. **6** You should take your spare pair in case
your glasses get broken. **7** We're taking our autograph book with
us in case we meet someone famous. **8** They packed a couple of
umbrellas in case it rained.

Writing

3 **1** Sir/Madam **2** apply for **3** advertised in **4** I am very
interested in travel **5** I would be suitable for the job **6** motivated
me to have confidence in my own abilities **7** fluent Spanish
8 I have an extensive knowledge **9** be willing to move
10 I can be contacted

Review and consolidation unit 2

Vocabulary

1

2 **1** sick **2** retirement **3** makes **4** on **5** work **6** made
7 promoted **8** from

Futures overview

3 **1** B **2** A **3** B **4** A **5** A **6** A

Future Perfect and Future Continuous

4 **1** will have cleaned **2** will be sunbathing **3** Will you be watching **4** will have repaired **5** will have travelled **6** Will you have finished **7** Will you be visiting **8** will be asking

Vocabulary

5 **1** b **2** c **3** f **4** d **5** e (not needed: a)

in case

6 (suggested answers) **1** I put on some insect repellent in case there were mosquitoes. **2** You'd better take an umbrella in case it rains. **3** I always keep some aspirin in case I get a headache. **4** I think you should put on some sun cream in case the sun is strong. **5** You should take a map in case you get lost.

Vocabulary

7 **1** (line 3) applied ~~to~~ for **2** (line 5) keen ~~of~~ on **3** (line 5) passionate ~~on~~ about **4** (line 11) different ~~at~~ from **5** (line 10) believe ~~to~~ in **6** (line 14) worry ~~of~~ about **7** (line 15) good ~~of~~ at **8** (line 16) proud ~~in~~ of

Unit 3 Old or new

Lesson 3.1
Listening

1a **1** 458 million **2** 1959 **3** directed **4** 1960 **5** 1961 **6** Spanish **7** actor **8** 1963 **9** starring **10** 2004

b **1** *Lawrence of Arabia* **2** *Spartacus* **3** *Ben Hur* **4** *Troy* and *Alexander* **5** *Cleopatra* **6** *Gladiator*

c **1** lying dormant **2** genre **3** re-examine **4** golden age **5** sets **6** superb **7** alongside **8** fortune **9** attendances **10** extras

Grammar: narrative tenses

2 **1** has been **2** made **3** had **4** had taken **5** was **6** appeared **7** had never appeared **8** came **9** was beginning **10** were earning

3 (suggested answers) **1** was eating **2** hadn't been/had never been **3** had been working **4** rained **5** had eaten **6** was released **7** had been lying **8** met

Vocabulary: time expressions

4 **1** For the previous **2** since then **3** up until that point **4** throughout **5** at that time **6** from that point on **7** while **8** After that

Writing

5 (suggested answer)

Deborah loved her cat Tiddles very much so she was very upset when it went missing. She put up notices offering a reward for its return.

Mr and Mrs Branksome enjoyed watching television in the evenings, although their TV was very old.

One evening they were watching TV when they noticed there was something wrong with the picture on their television. Mr Branksome couldn't see anything wrong with the TV set.

They took a torch and went outside to find out if there was something wrong with the aerial.

They saw a cat at the top of the TV aerial so they phoned the fire brigade.

A firefighter on a long ladder managed to rescue the cat.

They returned the cat to Deborah and she gave them the reward.

They used the money from the reward to buy a brand-new television.

Lesson 3.2
Vocabulary: materials

1

Pronunciation

2 **1** The letter 'r' isn't pronounced. **2** No. **3** Yes. **4** Stress is on the first syllable.

Reading

3a **1** They are tiny shops that stay open late at night. **2** They are not staffed by local people. **3** People from the Indian sub-continent. **4** Members of the owner's family work there. **5** They share in the profits.

b **1** well-known **2** huge **3** city-dwellers **4** rarely **5** immigration **6** run **7** economics **8** source

Grammar: articles

4 **1** – **2** the **3** the **4** – **5** – **6** the **7** an **8** a **9** – **10** the

5 **1** ✓ **2** Janine and Mike have got **a** beautiful garden. **3** She'd been living in ~~the~~ Los Angeles since the 1980s. **4** ✓ **5** When I was young I wanted to be **an** astronaut. **6** Let's have another look at ~~a~~ **the** first one they showed us. **7** I think **the** mobile phone is the greatest invention ever. **8** ✓ **9** Rudolf's planning to study ~~the~~ philosophy at university. **10** Have you got ~~the~~ **a** double room with a sea view? **11** The Azores are in the middle of **the** Atlantic Ocean. **12** ✓ **13** I love looking at ~~a~~ **the** moon at night. **14** This is **the** most exciting book I've read for a long time. **15** ✓.

How to: communicate interactively

6 **1** feel **2** about **3** What **4** true **5** do **6** else

Lesson 3.3
Reading

1a **1** Zara **2** Shell **3** Gap **4** Nestlé **5** Gap **6** Shell **7** Coca-Cola **8** Zara **9** Gap **10** Coca-Cola

b **1** beverages **2** manufacturer **3** non-alcoholic **4** founded **5** distributor **6** brands **7** worldwide **8** consume

Grammar: adjectives and adverbs

2 **1** When I have a bad headache all I want to do is lie down. **2** He didn't work hard so he was bound to fail the exam. **3** You're very early; did you drive fast? **4** Anna is always expensively dressed in designer outfits. **5** The clients will certainly expect to get a discount. **6** It snowed heavily throughout our holiday. **7** He rudely interrupted me in the middle of my speech. **8** Do you know them well? **9** I'm definitely going to take the First Certificate exam this year. **10** The weather can be surprisingly hot in September.

3 **1** reasonably priced **2** completely ruined **3** recently **4** hard **5** well **6** probably **7** nearly **8** unlikely **9** late **10** high

Vocabulary: verb phrases with *take*

4 **1** C   **2** C   **3** A   **4** A   **5** C   **6** B   **7** C   **8** A

Review and consolidation unit 3

Narrative tenses

1 **1** had been cleaning   **2** invaded   **3** were playing/played   **4** had been waiting   **5** had started   **6** was built   **7** were watching   **8** had taken   **9** had been working   **10** was having

Vocabulary

2 **1** e   **2** j   **3** a   **4** l   **5** f   **6** h   **7** d   **8** k   **9** b   **10** g
11 c   **12** i

3 (crossword)

Across: **4** TRADITIONAL   **5** PREVIOUS   **6** ANCIENT   **8** DURING   **9** ELDERLY
Down: **1** FASHIONED   **2** INSTINCT   **3** FASHIONABLE   **6** ANTIQUE   **7** CENTURY

Articles

4 **1** the most   **2** Portsmouth   **3** the railway   **4** a tunnel
5 the longest   **6** ships   **7** the United States   **8** the Atlantic
9 a ship   **10** a propeller   **11** Ambition   **12** stubbornness

Adjectives and adverbs

5 **1** ~~lately~~ late   **2** ✓   **3** ~~general~~ generally   **4** ~~finely~~ fine
5 ~~quick~~ quickly   **6** ~~hardly~~ hard   **7** ✓   **8** ~~interestingly~~ interesting
9 ~~highly~~ high   **10** ~~definite~~ definitely

6 **1** The professor treats all his students in a friendly way.
2 Isabel is definitely the oldest student in our class.   **3** I washed the sheets this morning.   **4** My brother sometimes forgets his PIN number.   **5** Daniela left her suitcase in the corner of the room.
6 The children stupidly forgot to bring their swimming costumes.
7 He wasn't driving dangerously, but he was going quite fast.
8 She has a warm and caring personality.

Vocabulary

7 **1** away   **2** in   **3** stride   **4** over   **5** for   **6** in   **7** to   **8** off

8 **1** Emma loves motherhood.   **2** Friendship is the most important thing for Pepe.   **3** David is a pianist.   **4** We need to increase production/productivity.   **5** Happiness is more important than wealth.   **6** I'm not very pleased with the arrangement.   **7** Professor Grant is an inventor.   **8** Children love excitement.   **9** There is a lot of crime in this neighbourhood.   **10** My brother is a physicist.

Unit 4 Risk

Lesson 4.1
Reading
1a 3

b **1** F   **2** T   **3** F   **4** T   **5** F   **6** F   **7** T   **8** T
c **1** i   **2** e   **3** d   **4** h   **5** c   **6** g   **7** j   **8** a   **9** f   **10** b

Grammar: *If* structures (1)

2 **1** If I get a laptop, I'll be able to send emails when I'm travelling.   **2** If the train comes on time, I won't be late for my interview.   **3** If Maribel passes the driving test, she'll buy a car.   **4** If I lived near a pool, I'd swim more often.   **5** If Terry wasn't/weren't scared of flying, he would travel around the world.
6 If Celia could sing, she would join a choir.   **7** If Dave hadn't known all the answers, he wouldn't have won the prize.   **8** If Helena hadn't lost the tickets, she would have gone to the concert.   **9** If Malik's sales figures hadn't been disappointing, he might have got a promotion.   **10** If we hadn't had to queue up for tickets, we wouldn't have missed the start of the show.

3 **1** would/'d like   **2** wouldn't have happened   **3** had/'d been
4 would have told   **5** phone   **6** will/'ll be able   **7** doesn't have
8 will not/won't know   **9** finds   **10** will/'ll contact

Lesson 4.2
Vocabulary: physical movements

1 **1** landed   **2** leap   **3** lean   **4** bend   **5** tuck   **6** balance
7 roll   **8** swinging

Writing: explaining how to do something

2 (suggested answers)
- Take out the spare tyre and put it on the ground.
- Take out the jack and the wrench.
- If your wheel has a cover, remove it.
- Use the wrench to loosen the nuts slightly.
- Position the jack according to the instructions in your car owner's manual.
- Raise the car about 10 centimetres off the ground by turning the handle on the jack
- Now use the wrench to completely unscrew the nuts.
- After removing the nuts pull the wheel off.
- Put the wheel in the boot.
- Lift up the spare wheel and slip it into position
- Put the nuts back and tighten them up by hand – don't use the wrench.
- Lower the car back on to the ground.
- Use the wrench and turn the nuts clockwise as hard as you can.
- Replace the wheel cover if you've got one.
- Put the jack, the wrench and the old wheel in the boot.

Listening and grammar: expressing obligation

3a **1** A mobile phone camera.   **2** He puts it in front of his face.
3 She was too close/was supposed to be further away.
4 He doesn't understand how Alice can see the photo so quickly.
5 You had to take the film to be processed before you could see the photos.

b **1** A   **2** A   **3** G   **4** G   **5** A

4 **1** don't have to   **2** Should   **3** needn't   **4** mustn't
5 supposed to be   **6** Don't you have to   **7** had to   **8** shouldn't

5 **1** picture, print   **2** process, develop   **3** flash
4 out of focus   **5** digital

6 **1** ~~should~~ shouldn't   **2** ✓   **3** ~~mustn't~~ needn't /don't have to   **4** ~~Must you~~ Did you have to   **5** ✓
6 ~~should~~ have to   **7** ~~needn't~~ mustn't   **8** ~~shouldn't~~ should

Lesson 4.3
Reading
1a 3

b **1** eight   **2** tickets and a full schedule of events   **3** yes   **4** 25
5 £20

c **1** your chance to turn fantasy into thrilling reality   **2** leading
3 longing for   **4** closely-guarded   **5** thrilling   **6** humdrum
7 predictable   **8** instructors

Grammar: emphasis

2 **1** I do like your new suit.   **2** Amanda does complain a lot.
3 He did say he was sorry several times.   **4** I did ask the boss for permission.   **5** We do know what we are talking about.

3 **1** really   **2** so   **3** much   **4** such   **5** very   **6** just   **7** so
8 really

4 **1** It's Chinese food that they love.   **2** It was his assistant that she spoke to.   **3** It was the first film that I didn't like.   **4** It's my thumb that hurts, not my finger.   **5** It's modern poetry that Clara really doesn't like.   **6** It's his attitude that I really don't understand.

Pronunciation

5 **1** yesterday   **2** black   **3** hall   **4** left   **5** Jane

Vocabulary: phrasal verbs with *out*

6a **1** find   **2** run   **3** turned   **4** give   **5** sort
b **1** ~~took~~ turned   **2** ✓   **3** ~~put~~ sort   **4** ✓   **5** ~~fall~~ put
6 ~~turns~~ sorts

Review and consolidation unit 4

Vocabulary

1 **1** endurance   **2** ambition   **3** gamble   **4** luck   **5** dream
6 substantial   **7** incredibly   **8** opportunity

If structures (1)

2 **1** C   **2** B   **3** B   **4** A   **5** B   **6** A   **7** C   **8** B

Vocabulary

3 **1** swing   **2** stretch   **3** roll   **4** lean   **5** balance   **6** land
7 tuck   **8** bend

Expressing obligation

4 **1** have   **2** mustn't   **3** shouldn't   **4** was supposed to
5 ought to   **6** don't have to   **7** should have   **8** ought to
9 mustn't   **10** needn't

Emphasis

5 **1** It was the shellfish that made me feel sick.   **2** She did try to contact you.   **3** I really, really admire people who do voluntary work.   **4** It is my left leg that I injured.   **5** Gerald is such a good footballer.   **6** Henrietta does give a lot of money to charity.
7 It was my mobile phone that was stolen.   **8** My new computer was very, very expensive.   **9** Javier did do a lot of work for us.
10 It is his wife that does most of the housework.

6 **1** that   **2** does   **3** so   **4** It   **5** did   **6** really   **7** such   **8** is

Vocabulary

7 **1** works out   **2** put out   **3** find out   **4** run out   **5** sort out   **6** fell out   **7** gave out   **8** turned out
8

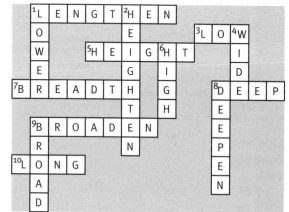

Unit 5 The past

Lesson 5.1
Listening

1a (suggested answers)   **1** Joe made TV commercials and short films.   **2** A lot of money is involved.   **3** There isn't much contact with accountants.   **4** The distances are enormous so you have to drive to the shops.   **5** They'd usually walk to do their shopping.   **6** Sunny weather.

b **1** How long has Joe been in the US?   **2** How old was he when he came to the US?   **3** Why did he choose to live in the States?
4 How many films has Joe made in the US?   **5** What is different about film-making in the US?   **6** What does his wife miss?
7 Why do people have to drive everywhere/to the shops?
8 Why didn't they do much filming outdoors in England?

c **1** melting pot   **2** studio executives   **3** drive somebody mad   **4** to be on top of somebody   **5** location work

Grammar: *used to /get used to /would*

2 **1** used to   **2** would/'d / used to   **3** would /'d/ used to
4 didn't use to   **5** getting used to   **6** would/'d   **7** didn't use to
8 am/'m used to

3 **1** A✓B✗C✓   **2** A✓B✗C✓   **3** A✓B✓C✓   **4** A✗B✓C✗
5 A✓B✗C✓   **6** A✗B✓C✓   **7** A✗B✓C✓   **8** A✓B✓C✗
9 A✗B✓C✗   **10** A✗B✓C✗

Vocabulary: appearance
4

<table>
<tr><td colspan="8"></td><td>¹M</td></tr>
<tr><td>²W</td><td>A</td><td>V</td><td>Y</td><td></td><td></td><td></td><td></td><td>U</td></tr>
<tr><td>R</td><td></td><td></td><td></td><td></td><td></td><td></td><td></td><td>S</td></tr>
<tr><td>I</td><td></td><td></td><td></td><td></td><td></td><td></td><td></td><td>C</td></tr>
<tr><td>N</td><td></td><td></td><td></td><td></td><td></td><td></td><td></td><td>U</td></tr>
<tr><td>K</td><td></td><td>³D</td><td></td><td></td><td></td><td>⁴S</td><td>L</td><td>I</td><td>⁵M</td></tr>
<tr><td>L</td><td></td><td>Y</td><td></td><td>⁶T</td><td>⁷S</td><td>A</td><td></td><td>O</td></tr>
<tr><td>⁸E</td><td>L</td><td>E</td><td>G</td><td>A</td><td>N</td><td>T</td><td>R</td><td>U</td></tr>
<tr><td>S</td><td></td><td>D</td><td></td><td>N</td><td>O</td><td></td><td>S</td></tr>
</table>

(crossword: WAVY, WRINKLED, DYED, SLIM, ELEGANT, TANNED, SCRAWNY, MUSCULAR, MOUSY, CURLY, BALD)

Lesson 5.2
Reading

1a 3

b **2** They drive into the suburbs of Milan.   **3** A motorbike crashes into the back of their car.   **4** They get out of their car to see what has happened.   **5** Two Italian men drive off in their Mercedes.   **6** They walk around trying to find a police station.   **7** They get into an Italian police car.   **8** They have to wait while the police officer deals with an accident.   **9** The police take Dieter and Kirsten to the railway station.   **10** They catch the slow train back to Zürich.   **11** The Italian men steal everything from their house and drive away in a van.   **12** Dieter and Kirsten get back to their house in Zürich.

c **1** convertible   **2** set off   **3** rushing   **4** sprawled   **5** groaning   **6** spending spree   **7** flag (it) down   **8** exhausted   **9** lent   **10** removal truck

Grammar: expressing ability

2 **1** wasn't very good at **2** could **3** could **4** knew how to
5 couldn't **6** manage to **7** couldn't **8** be able to
9 succeeded in **10** managed to

3 **1** able **2** succeed **3** be **4** at **5** Could **6** good/great
7 managed **8** how **9** will **10** terrible

How to: talk about memories

4 **1** They went to the seaside in summer, not winter. **2** They had picnics on the beach, not in the forest. **3** There are two sisters, not three. **4** They are serving food to the father, not other way around.

Lesson 5.3
Vocabulary: feelings

1 **1** relieved **2** curious **3** confused **4** excited **5** annoyed
6 suspicious **7** shocked **8** sceptical

2 **1** uninterested **2** excited **3** optimistic **4** uneasy
5 suspicious **6** relieved

Reading

3a **1** F **2** H **3** A **4** E **5** D **6** B (unnecessary extracts are C and G)

b **1** He was smartly dressed but his clothes were soaking wet.
2 Although he can't speak, the missing man can play the piano.
3 He was wearing a suit. However, the labels were missing.
4 He had no obvious injuries. Nevertheless, he seemed confused.
5 Though he can't write words, he can draw pictures.
6 He may be an illegal immigrant. However, the police think he may be a professional musician.

c **1** d **2** h **3** f **4** j **5** g **6** a **7** i **8** c **9** e **10** b

Pronunciation

4b **1** /d/ **2** /d/ **3** /ɪd/ **4** /d/ **5** /t/ **6** /ɪd/

Grammar: although/but/however/nevertheless

5 **1** but **2** Nevertheless **3** Although/Even though **4** However
5 even though/although

6 **1** The children we met were healthy but very badly educated.
2 I've been to New York, although I've never seen the Statue of Liberty. **3** Your visa has expired. Nevertheless, we are prepared to allow you to stay for a further three months. **4** I hear Austria is great for skiing holidays, though I've never been there myself.
5 Even though I've lived in London for four years, I still get lost on the underground system. **6** My grandparents were poor but happy. **7** Although we enjoy long walks, we do find them quite tiring. **8** Pets are not usually permitted in the hotel. However, in this case we can make an exception.

Review and consolidation unit 5

Vocabulary

1 **1** B **2** A **3** B **4** C **5** A **6** B

used to/get used to/would

2 **1** Are you getting used to life in the big city? **2** Sally didn't use to have any friends when she was a child. **3** I would go to the library every morning when I was a student. **4** The company used to export cars to Asia. **5** Did he get used to the software fairly quickly? **6** When I was young I didn't use to watch much television. **7** How often would you get the bus to school?
8 I've got used to staying up late. **9** It was easy to get used to the new computer. **10** Pepe didn't use to live in a big house.

Vocabulary

3 **1** clean-shaven **2** wrinkles **3** bald **4** wavy/curly
5 muscular **6** scruffy **7** mousy **8** good-looking **9** dyed
10 round

Expressing ability

4 **1** was able to repair/managed to repair/succeeded in repairing
2 could play **3** won't be able to come **4** good at/great at cooking
5 Did you manage to/Did you succeed in finding/Were you able to find
6 will be able to type

Vocabulary

5

```
          ¹U        ²S C E P T I  ³C A L
  ⁴A      N         U            O
  N       I         S            N
  N       N         P            F
  ⁵O P T  I M I S T I C          U
  Y       E         C            S
  E       ⁶R E L I  E V E D      E
  D       E         O            D
          S    ⁷C U R I O U  ⁸S
          T         S        H
          E                  O
          D              ⁹E X C I T E D
                            K
                    ¹⁰U N E  A S Y
                            D
```

although/but/however/nevertheless

6 **1** B **2** A **3** A **4** B **5** A **6** A **7** B **8** A

7 **1** ~~of~~ in **2** ~~position~~ place **3** no mistakes **4** ~~a nail~~ nails
5 ~~know everything~~ know-all **6** no mistakes
7 ~~high-flying~~ high-flyer **8** ~~awkward custom~~ awkward customer

Unit 6 Explore

Lesson 6.1
Reading

1a **2**

b (suggested answers) **1** How long have Chinese 'speed tourists' been coming to Germany? **2** How many tourists are expected to arrive this year. **3** What is it that tempts the Chinese tourists to drive on the autobahns? **4** How many kilometres of German motorways have no speed limit? **5** What makes/types of car do the tour operators offer to the tourists? **6** What speed are these cars capable of?/How fast can these cars go? **7** How much does a six-day autobahn tour cost? **8** How many people die on China's roads each day?

c **1** holidaymakers, travellers **2** autobahns, motorways, highways
3 tour operators **4** virtually **5** mythical **6** undeterred

Grammar: Present Perfect Simple and Continuous

2 **1** have been flocking **2** have added **3** have been bringing
4 have discovered **5** has been expanding **6** has not proved
7 have reacted **8** have been

3 **1** No, I haven't paid for the shopping yet. **2** They've been swimming in the lake. **3** No, I've never been/gone there.
4 Yes, he's just come back from Miami Beach. **5** I've been following a strict diet for the last two months. **6** No, I've already done it.
7 Yes, she's been typing it since lunchtime. **8** Yes, I've been teaching karate for more than ten years. **9** I've been washing the floors all afternoon. **10** No, I haven't been a member since 2004.

Vocabulary: adjectives with -ed/-ing endings

4 **1** annoyed, annoying **2** inspiring, inspired
3 fascinating, fascinated **4** petrified, petrifying
5 daunting, daunted

Lesson 6.2
Reading
1a **1** F **2** C **3** G **4** E **5** A

b **1** T **2** T **3** F **4** F **5** F **6** T **7** T **8** F

c Built entirely centrally heated formerly known
sparsely populated surprisingly relaxing reasonably comfortable
well stocked

Vocabulary: weather
2

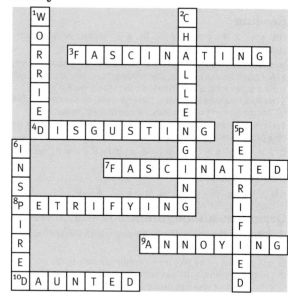

Grammar: questions
3 **1** (had) h **2** (did) e **3** (did) j **4** (How) a **5** (Did) g
6 (Who) i **7** (long) c **8** (was) b **9** (Was) f **10** (Are) d

4 **1** Who was she talking to? **2** Do you know if this is my seat?
3 Can you tell me how much it costs? **4** Where did they take the
car? **5** Could I ask you to open the window? **6** How do you turn
off the computer? **7** Are these the correct answers? **8** How long
have you been working here?

5 **1** Can you tell me what your email address is? **2** Could I ask
you if/whether Graham Randall lives here? **3** Do you know if this
is the correct platform for the train to Brighton? **4** I'd like to know
which seats in the plane have got the most legroom. **5** Can I ask
you if/whether the doctor is available now? **6** Can you explain
exactly where she lives? **7** Do you know how much the tickets
cost? **8** Would you tell me who is in charge?

Lesson 6.3
Listening
1a **A** 4 **B** 3 **C** 1 **D** 5 **E** 2

b **1** 5 **2** 4 **3** 2 **4** 3 **5** 1

c **1** considered **2** uproot **3** intrigued by **4** grim **5** tempting
6 to be honest **7** obviously **8** opportunities

Vocabulary: verb phrases about moving/travelling
2 **1** g **2** c **3** f **4** a **5** h **6** e **7** d **8** b

Grammar: comparative & superlative adjectives and adverbs
3 **1** more exciting than **2** The biggest **3** greater than
4 the most expensive **5** isn't as long **6** the fastest **7** the tallest
8 shorter than

4 **1** most heavy heaviest **2** is bit is a bit **3** bad hurt badly hurt
4 lately late **5** is most is the most **6** hoter hotter **7** than as
8 quite lot quite a lot **9** more far farther/further **10** taller tall
11 good well **12** most bad worst

Pronunciation
5a **1** All the underlined sounds are the same (/ə/ schwa)
2 All the underlined sounds are different /ə/, /æ/, /ə/, /ɑː/.

b **1** D **2** S **3** S **4** S **5** D

Review and consolidation unit 6
Vocabulary
1 **1** independence independent **2** shocked shock
3 make have **4** journey travel **5** through into **6** wonder wander

Present Perfect Simple and Continuous
2 **1** has been **2** has become **3** has been leading/has led
4 has been appearing **5** has had **6** helped **7** has given
8 has visited **9** have clearly influenced **10** met **11** spoke
12 has only been doing

Vocabulary
3

4 **1** e **2** h **3** a **4** f **5** c **6** g **7** d **8** b

Questions
5

(line 4) Where went you for your holidays? → Where did you go ...

(line 6) Who did go on holiday with you? → Who went on holiday ...

(line 8) Can I ask what is her name? → Can I ask what her name is?

(line 10) Could you tell me what does she for a living? → what she
does for a living ...

(line 15) Can you tell me is she British? → ... if/whether she is British.

(line 17) How long she has lived here? → ... has she lived here?

(line 19) I'd like to know where did you meet her. → ... where you
met her.

(line 25) Would you tell me how long did you stay in Florida? → ...
how long you stayed ...

Vocabulary
6 **1** move **2** off **3** abroad **4** emigrated **5** around **6** set
7 home **8** off **9** away **10** walked

Comparative & superlative adjectives and adverbs
7 **1** A✓ B✗ C✗ **2** A✗ B✓ C✗ **3** A✓ B✗ C✗ **4** A✗ B✗ C✓
5 A✓ B✗ C✗ **6** A✓ B✗ C✓ **7** A✗ B✗ C✓ **8** A✗ B✓ C✗

8 **1** for **2** have **3** make **4** without **5** back **6** lengths
7 on **8** the

Unit 7 Excess

Lesson 7.1
Listening

1a **1** Three. **2** Which take-away restaurant to go to.
3 To go to the Chinese take-away.

b **1** Alice **2** Ben **3** Tom **4** Alice **5** Ben **6** Alice **7** Ben
8 Tom

c **Feeling very hungry:** starving, ravenous, I could eat a horse
Positive opinion: yummy, delicious, scrumptious
Negative opinion: not too keen on, disgusting, greasy, to be sick of
something, tasteless

Grammar: countable and uncountable nouns

2 **1** C **2** B **3** A **4** C **5** B **6** A **7** A **8** C **9** A **10** C
3 **1** A✗ B✓ **2** A✓ B✓ **3** A✓ B✗ **4** A✗ B✓ **5** A✓ B✗
6 A✓ B✓

Vocabulary: food and cooking

4a an electric cooker grilled sausages grated cheese
a wooden spoon a talented cook a complicated recipe
scrambled eggs a china plate sour milk a frying pan

b **1** grated cheese **2** an electric cooker **3** grilled sausages
4 scrambled egg **5** a talented cook **6** sour milk

Lesson 7.2
Reading

1a 2

b **1** d **2** f **3** a **4** g **5** c **6** b **7** h **8** e

c **1** valuable **2** argue **3** rival **4** follow his lead **5** impact
6 masterpieces **7** recession **8** wholly

Vocabulary: verb phrases about money

2 **1** ~~refund~~ receipt **2** ~~bargain~~ discount **3** ~~haggling~~ bidding
4 ~~worth~~ afford **5** ~~bidding~~ haggling **6** ~~afford~~ worth

Grammar: passives

3 **1** was created **2** was taken over **3** had started **4** scored
5 organised **6** had been sold **7** were invited **8** was bought

4 **2** The metal strips are fed into a cutting machine. **3** The metal
is cut into round shapes called 'blanks'. **4** After they have been
cut out the blanks are heated in a furnace. **5** The blanks are
washed while they are being heated./While they are being heated
the blanks are washed. **6** each coin is stamped with a pattern on
both sides. **7** The coins are cooled and counted. **8** The coins are
distributed to the banks.

5 **1** Alison has been given a prescription. **2** The present
mustn't be opened until your birthday. **3** The crime is
being investigated. **4** The hotel is going to be opened in
November. **5** The children will be driven to the party.
6 My house can be seen from the top of the hill. **7** They were being
watched. **8** That DVD hasn't been released yet. **9** The burglar
might have been seen. **10** Nothing was taken.

Writing/How to: a letter of complaint

6 (suggested answer)

> Dear Sir/Madam,
>
> I am writing to complain about a mobile phone I bought in your
> shop on 6th January.
>
> When I got home I was shocked to find that it did not work,
> especially as it cost €250.
>
> I would be grateful if you could send me another phone. If this is
> not possible, I would like a full refund of my money as soon as
> possible.
>
> I look forward to hearing from you.
>
> Yours faithfully,
>
> Mandy Smith

Lesson 7.3
Listening

1a **1** goldfish **2** dog **3** snake **4** horse **5** cats

b **1** dog **2** horse **3** fish **4** dog **5** horse **6** cats
7 snake **8** horse

c **Ways animals move:** trot, dart, crawl
Places animals live: tank, stable, kennel
Animal characteristics: sinuous, playful, gentle

Grammar: *have/get something done*

2 **1** has her hair done **2** has his car washed **3** have their
house painted **4** has here eyes tested **5** has his blood pressure
checked **6** have our boiler serviced

3 **1** The bag got left behind. **2** Linda has her clothes washed
(by the maid). **3** I have my post forwarded (to me). **4** Will you get
your hair cut this week? **5** How often do you have your windows
cleaned? **6** I should have my homework done by six o'clock.

Vocabulary: animals and animal expressions

4

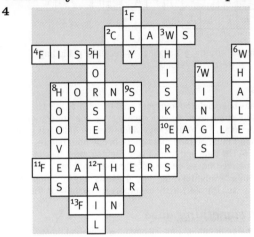

Pronunciation

5 **1** cow **2** beak **3** tiger **4** eagle **5** fur

Review and consolidation unit 7

Vocabulary

1 **1** luxury **2** extravagant **3** far-fetched **4** spending
5 overpriced **6** extra-large

Countable and uncountable nouns

2 **1** ~~luggages~~ luggage **2** ✓ **3** ~~many~~ much **4** ~~little~~ a little
5 ~~a lots~~ a lot OR a lots **6** ~~a few~~ a little **7** ✓ **8** ~~a~~ spaghetti OR
(some) spaghetti **9** ~~few~~ a few **10** ~~much~~ many

Vocabulary

3

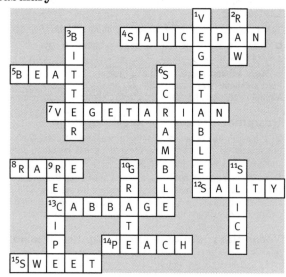

4 **1** bargain **2** afford **3** haggling **4** receipt **5** bidding
6 discount **7** worth **8** refund

Passives

5 **1** €450 has been debited from your credit card. **2** 128 KB protection software is used for your security. **3** Your itinerary is being sent by email. **4** Your tickets will be sent by first class post. **5** Your passport must be brought to check-in one hour before departure. **6** The date and time of your flights cannot be changed. **7** Seats can be pre-booked on the website. **8** Smoking is not allowed on any GoAway Travel flights. **9** Meals may be purchased on the plane. **10** Transfers from the airport are included in the price.

have/get something done

6 **1** had **2** got/been **3** (dry-)cleaned **4** have/get
5 repaired/fixed/mended **6** got/was **7** get/have
8 done **9** taken/printed/copied **10** having/getting

Vocabulary

7a **1** fin **2** beak **3** paws **4** hooves

b **1** bear, sore **2** blind, bat

8 **1** reheat **2** multinational **3** extra-large **4** uncomfortable
5 bilingual **6** overtired **7** ex-boyfriend **8** monotonous
9 undercooked **10** multipurpose

Unit 8 Success

Lesson 8.1
Reading

1a **1** D **2** F **3** A **4** H **5** B **6** E
b **1** F **2** T **3** T **4** T **5** F **6** T **7** F **8** T
c

1869	born in Porbandar, western India
1893	qualified as a lawyer
1915	returned to India, determined to fight against colonialism
1947	India gained independence
1948	assassinated by a Hindu fanatic

Grammar: *It's time/I'd rather/I'd better*

2 **1** A **2** B **3** B **4** B **5** B **6** A **7** A **8** A

3 **1** It's high time you moved to a bigger flat. **2** You'd better take an umbrella. **3** I'd rather go to the cinema. **4** It's about time John got a better computer. **5** Would you like me to bring my camera/ Would you rather I brought my camera? **6** I'd rather she didn't smoke. **7** I'd rather not work at the weekend. **8** You'd better have the salad.

Vocabulary: describing personality

4

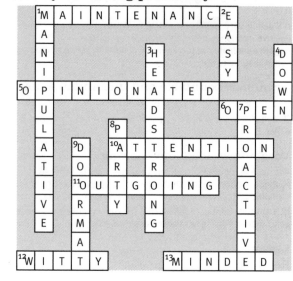

Lesson 8.2
Listening

1a **1** They are in a gym. **2** She is a trainer/fitness instructor. **3** To get fit, lose weight and improve his energy levels.

b **1** six **2** five **3** awfully **4** still **5** feels **6** energy
7 lethargic/tired **8** nutrition

c **1** complain **2** remind **3** ask **4** suggest **5** promise
6 explain **7** admit

Vocabulary: adjectives and intensifiers

2 See answers to Ex. 3b below.

Pronunciation

3a **1** When the children got back from the park they were <u>absolutely filthy</u>. **2** Clare was <u>really devastated</u> when she heard the news.

b **1** Saturday's game is <u>absolutely vital</u> for our hopes of promotion. **2** I always feel <u>really hungry</u> after swimming.
3 I often feel <u>really tired</u> at the end of the day. **4** Terry was <u>absolutely devastated</u> when the factory closed down. **5** Suzanne was <u>absolutely exhausted</u> after the race. **6** Poor Jo! He's <u>really upset</u> about his exam results. **7** What's there to eat? I'm <u>absolutely starving</u>! **8** Take your time to decide. This is a <u>really important</u> decision for you.

Grammar: reported speech

4 **1** Amanda suggested taking a short break then.
3 Amanda explained (that) it usually takes/took about three months to get fit. **4** Steven admitted (that) he was still eating desserts.
5 Steven asked (Amanda) if/whether she had prepared that nutrition sheet for him. **6** Amanda promised to do it the following week.

5 **1** C **2** A **3** B **4** B **5** A **6** A **7** C **8** B **9** B **10** A

6 **1** My brother suggested going out for a meal. **2** John explained that he couldn't come because he had to work that evening. **3** The children promised (that) they would never do it/that again. **4** The lifeguard warned (us) that swimming there could be very dangerous. **5** Maria admitted that she hadn't done her homework. **6** The customer decided to take the smaller model.

Lesson 8.3
Reading

1a 1 e **2** b **3** a **4** c **5** d

b 1 ~~this month~~ next month **2** ~~exam~~ practical **3** ~~five~~ nine
4 ~~maths~~ computer **5** ~~son~~ daughter **6** ~~The parents~~ Ryde
7 ~~older~~ younger **8** ~~few~~ most

c 1 e **2** h **3** b **4** j **5** a **6** d **7** i **8** f **9** c **10** g

Grammar: *hard* and *hardly*

2 1 hardly **2** hardly ever **3** hard **4** hardly anyone
5 hardly ever **6** hard **7** hardly anywhere **8** hardly anything
9 hardly **10** hardly anyone

3 1 hardly anyone **2** hard **3** hardly **4** hardly ever
5 hardly anything **6** hard

How to: give your opinion

4 1 think **2** concerned **3** believe **4** for **5** Firstly **6** in
7 because **8** then

Review and consolidation unit 8

Vocabulary

1 1 f **2** d **3** h **4** a **5** c **6** g **7** e **8** b

It's time/I'd rather/I'd better

2 1 time **2** rather **3** high/about **4** better **5** would/'d
6 phoned/called/spoke to/rang **7** had/'d **8** Would
9 not **10** be

Vocabulary

3 1 earth **2** headstrong **3** outgoing **4** manipulative **5** witty
6 doormat **7** proactive **8** centre **9** selfish **10** opinionated

4 1 upset **2** ✓ **3** clean **4** tiny **5** hot **6** ✓ **7** fascinating
8 ✓ **9** happy **10** freezing

Reported speech

5 1 [C] (that) the doctor was sick that day so he couldn't
see me. **2** [E] to do all the exercises on page 65 of the
Workbook. **3** [H] going to the cinema on Friday evening.
4 [A] not to touch those plates because they were very hot.
5 [I] stealing the money/(that) he had stolen the money.
6 [B] where my passport was. **7** [G] if/whether I was feeling
alright. **8** [J] to have the spaghetti Bolognese. **9** [D] to be at the
airport two hours before our departure. **10** [F] (that) she would pay
back the loan within six months.

hard and *hardly*

6 1 B **2** A **3** B **4** C **5** C **6** A **7** B **8** A **9** C **10** B

Vocabulary

7 1 look, to **2** cut, on **3** looking, to **4** put, with **5** come,
with **6** get, with **7** made, for **8** catch, with

Unit 9 Crime

Lesson 9.1
Vocabulary: law and insurance

1a 1 ~~convicted~~ sentenced **2** ~~fraud~~ arson **3** ~~sentenced~~ sued
4 ~~premium~~ fraud **5** ~~sued~~ convicted **6** ~~guarantee~~ appeal
7 ~~arson~~ premium **8** ~~appeal~~ guarantee

b 1 of **2** for **3** to **4** for

Reading

2a 1 F **2** D **3** C

b 1 What does cruise control do? **2** Why did the Mr Grazinski
step into the back of the motor home? **3** What injuries did
he suffer from? **4** Why did Kara Walton climb through the
window of the ladies toilet? **5** How much compensation was
she awarded? **6** How long had Terrence Dickson's career as a
burglar lasted? **7** Why was he trapped in the garage for eight
days? **8** What did he live on while he was trapped in the garage?

c Vehicles: cruise control, accelerator, speed, mph, owner's manual
Injuries/Harm: suffered, fell, broke, knocked out, starvation
Legal: court, awarded, compensation, expenses, jury

Grammar: sequencing devices

3 1 Having joined the motorway, he set the cruise control at 65 mph
and decided to step into the back of the motor home to make himself
a cup of coffee. **2** ... while struggling to get through the window
she fell to the floor and knocked out her two front teeth. **3** After
entering the garage from the house he realised the door could not be
opened from the inside.

4 1 A **2** B **3** A **4** A **5** B **6** A

5 1 Having told his best friend, Dave announced the news to his
colleagues. **2** After getting up, he went into the village to get some
food. **3** They watched the midnight movie before going to bed./
Before going to bed, they watched the midnight movie.
4 While (she was) watching TV Surinda heard a strange sound./
Surinda heard a strange sound while she was watching TV.
5 We went to the computer shop after reading lots of consumer
reports./After reading lots of consumer reports, we went to the
computer shop. **6** Having missed the bus, Jackie had to get a taxi.
7 My uncle started a new business after he had gone to America./
Having gone to America, my uncle started a new business.
8 The kids usually watch TV for an hour after doing their homework./
After doing their homework, the kids usually watch TV for an hour.

Lesson 9.2
Grammar: *must/might/can't have*

1 1 f **2** a **3** h **4** c **5** b **6** e **7** d **8** g

2 1 Somebody must have watered them. **2** She might not have
received the invitation. **3** He can't have gone out. **4** They must
have left already. **5** They can't have left the country. **6** He might
have forgotten to take it with him. **7** Maria must have passed the
exam. **8** You must have forgotten to bring it.

3 1 might have **2** must have **3** must have **4** can't have
5 might have **6** might have **7** must have **8** can't have

Vocabulary: compound adjectives

4 1 Mr Lockwood is middle-aged. **2** The chocolate cake is
home-made. **3** My sister works part-time. **4** The project was
time-consuming. **5** Elizabeth is single-minded. **6** I want a
one-way ticket to Hong Kong. **7** I had a last-minute change of
mind. **8** There's a brand-new hospital here.

Listening

5a 1 B **2** C **3** C **4** A **5** A

b 1 download **2** unravel **3** on behalf of **4** proportion
5 sort of **6** look like

c 1 on behalf of **2** look like **3** download **4** sort of
5 unravel **6** proportion

Lesson 9.3
Reading

1a 3

b 1 T **2** T **3** T **4** F **5** F **6** T **7** T **8** F

c 1 g **2** d **3** a **4** e **5** h **6** c **7** b **8** f

Grammar: relative clauses

2 1 1A 2B **2** 1B 2A **3** 1A 2B **4** 1A 2B

3 1 Miranda's boyfriend, who lives in Athens, is a doctor.
2 The house I'm living in is over a hundred years old. **3** Arthur
Conan Doyle, who was Scottish, was born in 1859. **4** The
government, which was elected last year, has introduced a new
tax. **5** Our local hospital, which is very old, is about to be closed
down. **6** The girl we met on holiday is coming to stay next weekend.
7 Spielberg's new film, which I saw yesterday, was fantastic.
8 The hotel we stayed in last summer had a heated swimming pool.

Pronunciation

4a **Sentences 1 and 3:** pause marks are correct because we pause at the beginning and end of non-defining relative clauses.

Sentence 2: the pause mark is not correct because we don't pause at the beginning of defining relative clauses.

b **1** We found our car ( ), which had been towed away two hours earlier ( ), at the police car pound.   **2** It was our car that had been towed away.   **3** The police took the car ( ), which had been blocking someone's gate ( ), to the car pound in Lennard Street.   **4** This is the gate that our car was blocking when it was towed away.

Review and consolidation unit 9

Vocabulary

1

A crossword puzzle with the following entries:
1 FINE
2 CLAIM
3 A...
4 S...
5 JUDGE
6 G...
7 C...
8 ROBBERY
9 T...
10 SENTENCE
11 A...
12 F...
13 FINGERPRINTS
14 PREMIUM

Sequencing devices

2 **1** leaving   **2** seen   **3** On   **4** After   **5** ran   **6** booking   **7** living   **8** Having   **9** finishing   **10** learned

must/might/can't have

3 **1** must have   **2** must have   **3** must have   **4** can't have   **5** might have   **6** might have

Vocabulary

4 **1** home-made   **2** brand-new   **3** one-way   **4** part-time   **5** left-handed   **6** last-minute   **7** time-consuming   **8** single-minded   **9** middle-aged   **10** so-called

Relative clauses

5 **1** My brother, who works in Cardiff, is an opera singer.   **2** Jenny, who/whom I told you about last week, is getting married.   **3** ✓   **4** The children that/who didn't pass the test had to take it again.   **5** Our car, which we bought last year, has been stolen from our garage.   **6** The film that was on TV last night was absolutely fascinating.   **7** ✓   **8** My colleague, who showed us how to use the computer, has been promoted to the Los Angeles office.

6 **2** It belonged to an old lady who died.   **3** When I was young the old lady, who used to be a schoolteacher, allowed me to play in her garden.   **4** The garden, which was huge, had lots of lemon trees.   **5** I used to pick the lemons from the trees that grew there.   **6** The old lady used the lemons (that) I had picked to make lemonade.

Vocabulary

7 **1** F   **2** T   **3** T   **4** T   **5** F   **6** T   **7** F   **8** F

Unit 10 Memories

Lesson 10.1
Listening

1a 2

b **1** Germany   **2** qualified   **3** Vienna   **4** magnetism   **5** Paris   **6** aristocrats   **7** king   **8** entertained   **9** forced   **10** 1815

c **1** A   **2** D   **3** A   **4** D   **5** C   **6** B   **7** B   **8** C

Vocabulary: belief and opinion

2 **1** ~~that~~ of   **2** ~~sceptie~~ sceptical   **3** is   **4** ~~convenienced~~ convinced   **5** ~~of~~ that   **6** ~~give~~ giving

Grammar: reflexive pronouns

3 **1** B   **2** C   **3** A   **4** C   **5** A   **6** C   **7** A   **8** C   **9** A   **10** B

4 **1** Darren cut himself while he was gardening.   **2** I made the cake myself.   **3** We've made all the arrangements ourselves.   **4** Mandy and Sylvia sent text messages to each other.   **5** My central heating turns itself on automatically if the temperature drops.   **6** The Bensons often send packages to themselves when they are abroad.   **7** Did you paint this picture yourself?   **8** Isabel works for herself.

How to: ask about other people's views

5 **1** Do you have any strong feelings about pollution?   **2** How do you feel about poverty?   **3** Are you for or against the death penalty?   **4** What are your views on fast food?   **5** What do you think of divorce?

Lesson 10.2
Reading

1a 2

b **1** F   **2** F   **3** T   **4** F   **5** T   **6** F   **7** F   **8** F

c **1** freshly baked   **2** optimistic   **3** pick up   **4** cash register   **5** subtly   **6** olfactory organs   **7** evocative   **8** harness

Vocabulary: advertising

2 **1** slogan   **2** makes   **3** classified ad   **4** target market

Pronunciation

3 (main stress underlined)
Three syllables: com<u>mer</u>cial, <u>cus</u>tomers, maga<u>zines</u>, persu<u>a</u>sion
Four syllables: ad<u>ver</u>tisement, infor<u>ma</u>tion, poli<u>ti</u>cians, <u>su</u>permarket

Grammar: gerunds and infinitives

4 **1** suggest   **2** joining   **3** writing   **4** her to get   **5** imagine   **6** speaking   **7** miss   **8** to come

5 **1** 1A 2B   **2** 1B 2A   **3** 1B 2A   **4** 1A 2B

Lesson 10.3
Reading

1a **1** D   **2** F   **3** A   **4** G   **5** B   (not needed: C, E)

b **1** What is removed from Joel's mind in the film?   **2** What do memory management drugs cause?   **3** How many of these drugs is the FDA currently testing?   **4** How does Derren Brown put ideas into people's minds?   **5** How can people be persuaded to carry out instructions without question?   **6** What has research shown us?

c **1** fiction   **2** neuroscientists   **3** compounds   **4** erase   **5** amazed   **6** manipulation   **7** orders   **8** carry out   **9** propaganda   **10** whim

Vocabulary: speaking

2

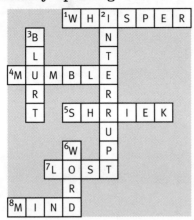

Crossword:
- 1 across: WHISPER
- 2 down: INTERRUPT
- 3 down: BLURT
- 4 across: MUMBLE
- 5 across: SHRIEK
- 5 down: SCRIPT
- 6 down: WORD
- 7 across: LOST
- 8 across: MIND

Grammar: *If* structures (2)

3a **1** c **2** f **3** d **4** a **5** g **6** e **7** h **8** b

b **1** mixed **2** zero **3** third **4** second **5** mixed

4 **1** If we hadn't gone to the sales, we wouldn't have bought an incredibly cheap sofa. **2** Charles wouldn't have overslept if he hadn't forgotten to turn on his alarm clock. **3** If you give plants water, they grow. **4** If I got a pay rise, I would be able to buy a nice house. **5** Don't use the generator unless there is a power failure. **6** Provided you pay by credit card, we will give you a guarantee. **7** You can have a party unless the neighbours complain. **8** As long as you show us a receipt, we can give you a refund.

Review and consolidation unit 10

Vocabulary

1 **1** unconscious **2** déjà vu **3** trust **4** premonition **5** mind **6** willpower **7** subconscious **8** persuasion

Reflexive pronouns

2 **1** ~~her~~ herself **2** ~~himself~~ him **3** ~~others~~ other **4** ✓ **5** ~~ourself~~ ourselves **6** ~~themselves~~ them **7** ✓ **8** repaired ~~me~~ repaired the broken chair myself

Vocabulary

3 **1** I am convinced that Jimmy is guilty of the crime. **2** Emily is in favour of longer prison sentences for criminals. **3** I reckon she could be our new manager. **4** I've always believed that people are basically honest. **5** Some politicians are against the new tax. **6** I'm sceptical about hypnosis.

4

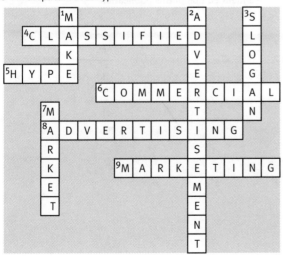

Crossword:
- 1 down: MK (MARKET)
- 2 down: ADVERTISEMENT
- 3 down: SLOGAN
- 4 across: CLASSIFIED
- 5 across: HYPE
- 6 across: COMMERCIAL
- 7 down: MARKET
- 8 across: ADVERTISING
- 9 across: MARKETING

Gerunds and infinitives

5 **1** to collect us **2** to turn on the burglar alarm **3** applying to universities **4** to inform you **5** working as a doctor **6** living there **7** eating the prawns **8** to have lunch **9** designing websites **10** me to take

Vocabulary

6 **1** d **2** a **3** h **4** g **5** f **6** c (not needed: b, e)

If structures (2)

7 **1** B **2** C **3** B **4** A **5** B **6** A **7** A **8** C **9** C **10** B

Vocabulary

8 **1** intelligence **2** psychologist **3** subconscious **4** their **5** responsibility **6** definitely **7** changeable **8** necessary **9** generous **10** occasionally

Pearson Education Limited,
Edinburgh Gate, Harlow
Essex, CM20 2JE, England
and Associated Companies throughout the world
www.longman.com

The right of Mark Foley to be identified as author of this work has
been asserted by him in accordance with the Copyright, Designs
and Patents Act 1988.

First published 2006
Third impression 2008

Set in 10.5/13pt Meta Plus book and 10/13pt Meta Plus Normal

Printed in Malaysia, KHL

ISBN 978-1-4058-2258-9 (Workbook with key and CD-ROM pack)
ISBN 978-1-4058-2693-8 (Workbook without key and CD-Rom pack)
ISBN 978-0-582-84636-4 (Workbook with key for pack)
ISBN 978-1-4058-2654-9 (Workbook without key for pack)
ISBN 978-1-4058-2250-3 (Workbook with key)
ISBN 978-0-582-84637-1 (Workbook without key)

Illustrated by: John Batten, David Shenton, Roger Wade-Walker

Photo Acknowledgements
We are grateful to the following for permission to reproduce photographs:
20th Century Fox / Ronald Grant Archive: pg72; **Buzz Pictures:** pg32(t); **Camera Press:** pg33(b); **Carolco Pictures /
Tristar Pictures / Ronald Grant Archive:** pg 80; **Coasterimage.com:** pg 49; **Corbis:** pg9, pg28, pg39; **Robert Harding
Picture Library:** pg 70; **Getty Images:** pg37(t), 60; **Sally & Richard Greenhill:** pg22, **Mike Gunnill:** pg 40; **Photofusion
Picture Library:** pg 37(b); **Punchstock:** pg33(t), 56 (Digital Vision), pg44 (Comstock) **Rex Features:** pg8; **By courtesy of
Sotheby's Picture Library, London:** pg 54; **Stockshot:** pg 32(b); **Topfoto:** pg 14; **Warner Bros TV / Bright / Kauffman /
Crane Pro / Kobal Collection / Chris Haston:** pg4; **www.icehotel.com:** pg 46 (Peter Grant).

Cover images by **Lonely Planet Images**(t) (Jonathan Swift), **Digital Vision**(l & b).

Picture research by Kevin Brown

Every effort has been made to trace the copyright holders and we apologise in advance for any unintentional omissions.
We would be pleased to insert the appropriate acknowledgement in any subsequent edition of this publication.

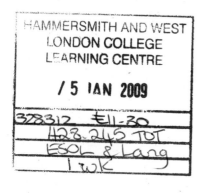